To Paul

With best wishes

from

Peter

ON THE CONSTITUTION

By the same author

A Sparrow's Flight
The Law of Arbitration
One Year's Work
The Law and Employers' Liability
The Times We Live In
Making Peace
The Left Was Never Right
The Purpose of Parliament
The Case for Conservatism
The Law of Monopolies, Restrictive Practices
and Resale Price Maintenance
The Conservative Case
Interdependence
Science and Politics
The Devil's Own Song
The Door Wherein I Went
Elective Dictatorship
The Dilemma of Democracy
Hamlyn Revisited: the British Legal System

LORD HAILSHAM

On The Constitution

HarperCollins*Publishers*

HarperCollins*Publishers*
77–85 Fulham Palace Road
Hammersmith, London w6 8jb

First published by HarperCollins*Publishers* 1992

1 3 5 7 9 10 8 6 4 2

Copyright © Lord Hailsham of St Marylebone, 1992

Lord Hailsham asserts the moral right to be
identified as the author of this work

A catalogue record for this book is
available from the British Library

ISBN 0 00 215998 8

Set in Linotron Janson by
Rowland Phototypesetting Ltd
Bury St Edmunds, Suffolk

Printed in Great Britain by
HarperCollinsManufacturing Glasgow

CONTENTS

I

Declaration at Customs

WITH A SMALL 'c' is this a conservative book. That is to say I believe in change which is cautious, continuous evolutionary, and carefully thought out, but in its consequences radical. But this work is no party political tract. It is based on a conviction that, over the centuries, the British Constitution has proved one of the most successful political structures ever devised by the wit of man. Today it is manifestly under strains. But these can be identified and discussed. There is plenty of life in the old dog left if we can avoid being stampeded into changes incompatible with its essential nature and genius. Throughout our history, our Constitution has proved flexible, sensitive and almost infinitely capable of evolutionary adaptation. It is under strain today mainly because it is over-centralised and subjected at its centre to an unacceptably high volume of work. For this there are two valid treatments. The first is to reduce the volume of work by attempting less and seeking to perform it more efficiently. The second is to attempt a certain degree of devolution both geographically and by function, without losing the advantage of a strong executive responsible to a single sovereign but elected legislature. We are approaching the limit of what can usefully be achieved in a unitary state. Most other nations of comparable size have, or have had imposed on them, some degree of federalism together with the rigidity of a written Constitution. Both would be foreign to our own traditional structure. The late A. V. Dicey identified as the twin pillars on which our Constitution rests, parliamentary sovereignty and the rule of law. He might, I believe, have added a third, which derived from its essentially flexible and evolving nature. This is our inveterate and, to my mind, highly desirable habit of being governed as much by convention as by the strict letter of the law. This is what makes the importation of foreign conceptions, American or continental, or otherwise alien constitutional language and thinking, into our constitutional debates so questionable. All may be admirable in themselves. But all are foreign to our way of doing things. Both may be admirable fruits, but you cannot graft a pear on a peach. I believe it may be possible to go forward on traditional lines by reducing the volume and pressure of work at the centre without surrendering what is of permanent value in our heritage.

It would be disingenuous to pretend that I can approach these matters without bringing with me a certain number of preconceptions, a kind of intellectual luggage which I am loath to describe as prejudices, but which I must expose at the customs barrier which confronts me before I approach my task.

Do I believe in freedom? Why, yes, of course. But I believe that freedom can exist only within a framework of enforceable law administered by an independent judiciary, and passed, or tacitly approved, by a legislature of two chambers supporting a strong executive responsible to it but at least in part controlling it. Of these two chambers, one is dominant because elected, and it is to this that the executive, individually and collectively, is primarily responsible. The other chamber, subordinate, but not for that reason by any means unimportant, supplies wisdom, experience, specialist knowledge and, above all, relaxed and civilised discussion. It must have powers sufficient to make the dominant chamber pause long enough to consider its reasoned argument, but not sufficient to override the powers of government or the considered wish of the electorate.

Do I believe in democracy? Yes, of course, but only as expressed through the framework of a Constitution such as I have described. Democracy is not the same as populism, which is and always has been one of its most dangerous enemies. Democracy should elect its leaders. But they should be leaders laying their case before public opinion for mature and serious discussion and not swayed by the knee-jerk reactions of opinion polls, which are no better than indicators, or of the media, which may change from day to day. Populism is the high road to incoherence, chaos, impotence and, ultimately, to authoritarianism of a kind which is the antithesis of democracy.

Do I believe in the separation of powers? Why, yes, but only as formulated in the way I have described. We have come a long way since the Glorious Revolution of 1688. The limited monarchy envisaged at the time William III came to the throne has given way to cabinet government, and, in addition to the separation of powers then envisaged between executive, legislature and judiciary, we have learned to separate the office of head of state, as personified by our hereditary monarchy, the focus of loyalty, the symbol of continuity, and the trustee of authenticity, from the head of government as personified by the Prime Minister, chairing and appointing members of a cabinet, all of whom, in contrast to the conception embodied in the American Constitution, are both members of one house or other of the legislature and responsible to them, and largely controlling, and partly controlled by, the majority party in the elected chamber.

I also believe in diversity in unity. Although not in any sense a supporter of either of the Unionist parties in Northern Ireland and no enemy to nationalist sympathies in Scotland, Ireland or Wales, I am unalterably attached to the United Kingdom of Great Britain and Northern Ireland. Although it was inevitable at the time, and is irreversible now, except in so far as the adverse effects can be mitigated by our common membership of the European Community, I bitterly regret the separation of the Republic of Ireland from the United Kingdom and its absence from the Commonwealth. My belief goes far deeper than regret at the existence of a land frontier in Ireland, the first in our history to exist since the Union of the two Crowns of England and Scotland after the death of Elizabeth I. I believe that all the peoples of this group of islands, from the Shetlands to Jersey, from County Kerry to Lindisfarne, if they are to enjoy any decent future at all or make any constructive contribution to Europe or the world, must transcend the differences of national cultures and religions, and must work together in harmony in good times and in bad. In that sense I am a Unionist through and through.

Obviously, in a work of this kind, there must be a certain amount of abstract academic discussion. But this is not intended as an academic enterprise. I believe that what I write will not be the worse for remaining essentially at the popular level. There will be no cross-references to the vast literature of learning available to the specialist in political and constitutional theory. These of course must form the staple fare of the serious student. My aim is humbler, but not, I trust, without value. It is to interest the general reader in the problems and development of our basic institutions. This can be no bad thing. Reform is in the air, and changes will come. But I make no apology for having turned down some of the most facile remedies as at best superficial and useless, and, at worst, damaging and capable of destroying what is most of value. I will, I trust, at least have stimulated interest and encouraged debate. The heaviest piece of luggage I have to declare is an unalterable belief in the value of objective analysis and civilised discussion. This needs no elaboration. But the absence of these in the past has been too often so disastrous as to make their declaration at the frontier an essential component of my crossing into the territory into which I now pass.

Before luggage is removed to the aircraft it must first be weighed. Some will require that I should discuss first principles, and then move on to facile conclusions, presenting an attractive whole and encouraging immediate and effective action. They will be disappointed, perhaps even repelled, by a more pedantic and pedestrian approach. I have attempted to analyse some of the factors which inhibit the rate and influence the cost of reforms which might otherwise be considered desirable. All reforms would have to be passed into legislation more or less under our existing rules, unless these can be changed in advance to overcome some of the difficulties involved in the passage through both Houses of Acts of Parliament all of which would have to take a certain precedence over urgent and indispensable measures of more immediate kind. One of the difficulties we still have to analyse consists in the fact that one of the permanent features of the constitutional process is the chronic shortage of parliamentary time which results in the indefinite postponement of measures crying out for action to meet the immediate legislative needs of a modern industrial society, and the unavoidable curtailment of discussion of any detailed measures which succeed in obtaining a place in the overburdened sessional programme of any given year.

The practical obstacles to reform are not to be swept aside as unworthy of consideration, even though they may themselves be part of the problem we are trying to solve.

It is also entirely unrealistic to disregard even the financial consequences of any change which might otherwise seem attractive to some in terms of principle. There may be, for example, many who look askance at the privileged position of the Church of England in the largest component part of the composite United Kingdom. It may be a trivial point, but our parish churches, cathedrals and national shrines are largely maintained in a usable condition by the offerings of the faithful. Before we turn all Jeffersonian overnight it might be worth considering whether and in what form the Consolidated Fund should be used to keep such an important factor in our architectural heritage, and to what alternative use the buildings could be put. In terms of practical politics, constitutional change is no more exempt from consideration of the art of the possible than any other sphere of public activity.

II

Fundamentals

I NOW APPROACH my main task. For years it has been apparent that our Constitution is under strain, and the perception of this fact has given rise to different prescriptions for change. This is healthy enough. No Constitution can be engraved on tablets of stone like those which Moses brought down from Sinai. As Burke put it, a nation which finds itself without the means of change will inevitably find itself without hope of survival. But successful prescriptions for treatment depend on accurate analyses of fact, that is, of the existing position. It is no good beginning with high-sounding generalities about inalienable rights or civil liberties or vain abstractions like 'the people' or 'society in general'. All too frequently, excessive concentration on generalities and first principles has led to incoherence or anarchy, and thence to dictatorship, without ever achieving the desirable end of civilised stability in which each individual and every minority group can enjoy in peace the fruits of their labour and leave at the end a decent and enhanced patrimony to family or successors. Unless accompanied by objective and scholarly thinking, starry eyes often end in floods of tears of grief and rage. Like patriotism, idealism is not enough.

The fact is that all freedom, all security, and the enjoyment of every human right derive from a condition of stability created and policed by the rule of law. In its origin, the rule of law derives from the claim by all political rulers, good or bad, liberal or authoritarian, to a monopoly or near monopoly of the use of force. This imposes on them all, irrespective of their class, not just the moral duty, but the practical necessity to police stability by imposing norms of conduct not only reflected in a criminal code, but extending to the settlement of all civil disputes between individuals who might otherwise be tempted to take the law into their own hands. This means the establishment of ordered government operating under a set of intelligible rules leading to predictable results. In the technical parlance of English law this is described by the concept of the King's (or Queen's) peace and the duty to maintain it. It is at this point that the moral ideas about justice begin to evolve. But, as Pontius Pilate might have asked, and Socrates constantly did, 'What is justice?' In constitutional terms, it is enough to say that in this sense justice involves at least four components. The first is a body of substantive and ascertainable rules of law, enforceable and effectively enforced. The second is an effective mechanism for the application of these general rules to the facts of the particular case. The third is a system of evidential and procedural rules to facilitate the ascertainment of the facts followed by the application to those facts of the rules of substantive law, and the fourth a body of individuals ('judges') who administer the system in case of dispute. A modern state usually distinguishes between the groups of persons who are responsible for the working of the several parts.

In our own society, which has passed through a great many phases in the course of a great many years, we usually recognise four separate groups. The first is the head of state ('the Sovereign') presiding over the whole and guaranteeing its legitimacy. The second includes the executive ('the government') operating the executive functions of government. The third is the judiciary for settling disputes and ordering the enforcement of the law, and the fourth is the legislature which changes or enacts the laws and defines the functions of the respective parts of the system. At the time when the United States Constitution was adopted in 1787, the functions of the head of state and the head of the executive government were not differentiated. This was because the founding fathers of that Constitution looked backwards for their inspiration to the Glorious Revolution of 1688 which treated King William III as head of the executive government and not merely head of state, and not forwards to cabinet government led by a Prime Minister. This differentiation the founding fathers wrongly regarded as a corrupt misuse of power, instead of recognising it, as they should have done, as the growing point of British institutions, and one which has actually proved the model for most other Constitutions of later date. Similarly, the American founders insisted on a rigid legal separation between the functions of legislature and executive government even to the extent that, by convention, no member of the President's cabinet may be a member of either House of Congress, whilst in most other countries of Western origin, all or most of the members of the executive at ministerial level have to be members of the legislature and are expected to command the confidence of at least the elected chamber within it.

In practice, the British model has changed its balance enormously during the course of the last two centuries. This is because our system of voting at elections as it has developed into universal adult suffrage favours, although it does not actually prescribe, a two-party system and, under such a system, retaining the confidence of parliament has come to mean in practice, though paradoxically, that the executive government controls the House of Commons far more obviously than that the House of Commons controls the executive. In practice, this has meant that enormous power is placed in the hands of the cabinet and, within the cabinet, of the Prime Minister, who in practice selects its members, distributes its offices amongst them, presides at meetings, constitutes its committees, and advises the head of state as to the exercise of the prerogative of dissolution. The absence of fixed term parliaments and of any constitutional limit on the ambit and content of any legislation which a parliament may enact together explain the distinctive features of the British Constitution as it has developed since 1688. These distinctive characteristics sharply differentiate our own constitutional arrangements both from the American model, where no President can exercise such influence, and from most of the characteristic types of Western European democracy where the two-party system is often the exception, and cabinets composed of more than one political group are almost the norm, and where many of the legislatures run for a fixed term rather than subject to a right of dissolution up to a maximum limit.

The same factors also explain, at least in part, why it is that the British Constitution is rather misleadingly referred to as 'unwritten' although from the Magna Carta to the Local Government Acts most of our constitutional law is contained somewhere in the growing volumes of written Acts of Parliament.

At this point, it is worth pausing for a moment to examine this last paradox at a little greater length. If a 'written' Constitution does not mean a Constitution wholly in writing, and an 'unwritten' Constitution does not mean a Constitution whose terms are not wholly or mainly written into the Statute Book, what meaning exactly is to be attached to either of these terms? The question is important because most of the 'Westminster model' Constitutions negotiated when each former colony became independent, are of the 'written' variety and, except in so far as they contain, as some do, a true federal element, a point to which we must return later, may be thought in general to conform broadly to the British model.

The answer is to be found not in the presence or absence of writing as such but in a limit on the nature of the laws which the courts will enforce, the forum to which constitutional disputes may be brought, and the mechanisms by which certain types of law may be amended or repealed. In countries in which the Constitution is 'written', there are effectively two types of law in force. These are first the general laws of the land and within the limits to which they must be confined, these are enacted or altered by the ordinary process of legislation passing through the ordinary legislatures and enforced by the ordinary courts of law. Secondly, quite separately from these, are the rules of constitutional law as contained in the 'written' Constitution, and these can only be amended or repealed by some special mechanism and, in the last resort, are not interpreted or applied by the ordinary courts but by a special Constitutional court or courts, like the Supreme Court of the United States, which have this power specifically conferred for the purpose. It is the coexistence of these two types of law within the same body politic which led the first Lord Birkenhead, in a case which came before the Privy Council in 1920, to rechristen the two types of Constitution 'controlled' and 'uncontrolled' instead of 'written' and 'unwritten'. I prefer myself to stick to the traditional nomenclature, since the use of the alternative is not merely confusing but wrongly implies that there are no effective checks and balances in our own 'unwritten' Constitution to control the misuse of power by its several parts. But it remains true that there is no legal limitation on the power of our own parliament to pass, amend or repeal any part of the law. We may alter the maximum duration of parliaments, the succession to the throne, or the identity of its occupant by precisely the same method as we can pass or change the laws regulating traffic or the possession of dangerous drugs. In fact we have done so in the Act of Settlement, in the act recognising the abdication of Edward VIII and in the successive acts passed during the last war prolonging the life of the parliament of 1935. It is an axiom of our constitutional law that no parliament may bind its successor, and the effect of these rules is that, at least in theory, there is no rule of customary or statute law which is immune to alteration or repeal by exactly the same process as other Acts of Parliament and that all rules of law, customary or enacted, are amenable to the ordinary courts and not by any special tribunal set up to try them.

A secondary result of all this is even stranger than might appear at first sight. In practice it has meant that the actual rules by which we are governed are often quite different from those which the courts are legally bound to enforce. In other words, in some fundamental respects, we are governed by conventional practices and not by law in its strict sense. It is for this reason as well as any others that our Constitution may be described as 'unwritten'.

A few obvious examples may suffice. It is an unalterable rule that the courts may only give effect to an Act of Parliament after it has received the Royal Assent. In other words the Sovereign has an uncontrolled veto on all Bills. But the formula of rejection (La Royne – or Le Roy – s'avisera) has never been used since the reign of Queen Anne, and, in the foreseeable future, must be regarded as obsolete. Similarly, in strict legal theory, the Queen could dismiss the Prime

development of party discipline in the House of Commons, and the decline of collegiality among ministers and the predominance of the Prime Minister's position within the cabinet must at least have altered its character in practice. It is clear that, valuable as it is as a shock absorber and guarantee of civilised standards, convention alone is an insufficient protection against the sheer volume of legislation and pressure of work at the centre engendered within the developments of the new Leviathan which is the modern state. This constitutes an agenda for a new scrutiny of our age-long institutions.

III

$\diamond\diamond\diamond$

Diversity in Unity

BEFORE I DEAL WITH the component parts of our truly remarkable, and highly successful, Constitution, I must insert a short discourse on one of the essential characteristics of a free society. Misused, our Constitution might easily be allowed to degenerate into an elective dictatorship. Even before the war, such respectable and democratic characters as the late Earl Attlee and Sir Stafford Cripps were openly toying with the idea of an enabling Bill, which would empower a newly elected left-wing government to bypass the dilatory parliamentary process of legislation through the two Houses and allow the executive in effect to legislate by decree. In making these suggestions these two eminent Labour leaders were clearly motivated by the belief that a radical new government would have so much to do that they could be held up in the doing of it by delaying tactics of a Conservative opposition. Happily their disastrous plan, based on a mistaken view of the nature of the Conservative party, was never carried into effect after their landslide victory in 1945, and the only miserable relic of it which actually reached the statute book was the Parliament Act of 1949. Partly their abandonment of these foolish and undemocratic ideas was assisted by the enormous scale of their majority in the Commons ('We are the masters

16

now') and partly to the increasing maturity of the Labour leadership after their experience of responsibility in the coalition cabinet. But that the project was at one time seriously discussed is also a reflection of the fact that Britain was already trembling on the brink of the size of unit which can easily be contained within the ambit of a unitary state, and a misunderstanding of the nature of popular sovereignty as enshrined in the ideals of a modern parliamentary democracy. Had the plan been carried out, we should have been right back to a legislation by proclamation as exemplified by Henry VIII and unsuccessfully attempted by the Stuarts and the Major Generals under Cromwell.

So far as a free and civilised society is concerned, pluralism, or rather diversity in unity, is the name of the game. The contrary view is now held only by the discredited Communists and the rather barmy fringe of the extreme left typified by the Militant Tendency, or, on the far right, by other extreme groups still happily unrepresented in parliament.

But there is more to the question than this. A total rejection of elective dictatorship involves a slightly deeper analysis of the nature of a civilised society under a constitutional government, whether this be limited by the letter of a written Constitution or by the restraining influence of convention and conventional wisdom.

Margaret Thatcher is credited with the dictum: 'Society does not exist'. Literally, of course, she was absolutely correct. Like all mere abstractions, 'Society' is a useful phrase but not a concrete reality. But there is danger in using the dictum without further analysis, since it encourages an equal and opposite fallacy, common to popular left and moderate right alike. This supposes that a nation is composed of a corporate entity (the state) and a collection of atomic units (the individual), each intent on pursuing his or her own individual sources of satisfaction, material or otherwise. A glance at the realities of life dismisses this over-simplification as a travesty of the facts. Like most other travesties, it is none the less dangerous for being absurd. It is a platitude, not less valuable for being obviously true, to repeat with Donne that no man is an island entire unto himself. We are all part of the main, and the main is a globe full of islands, continents, and oceans. We do not have to choose, as the Alternative Service Book of the Church of England foolishly suggests, between our own interests and the 'common good'. Some of an individual's interests are rights which in the furtherance of the 'common good' itself, ought to be defended by the full protection of the law. To override such rights in the interests of 'the people', 'the Reich', 'the working class' or whatever easy phrases a false ideology may choose to invent, is contrary to the 'common good'. It is as well to remember that the 'common good' is enriched rather than impoverished by the pursuit by individuals of what they perceive as their own legitimate interests, honourably and honestly pursued, and that law may include among its legitimate aims the protection of the individual or the minority against the majority or the state itself.

At a deeper level, however, the suggested dichotomy between the individual and society is basically flawed. Individuals do not exist as islands, entire unto themselves. They are born into families. They are nurtured in religions, ethnic groups, subordinate cultures. In our own islands, there are never plain British. They are English, Scots, Irish, Welsh, Jews and, more recently, Moslems, Asians and Africans, Chinese and Indians. Individuals use their rights of association to enter into partnerships, to form societies, professional associations, Trade Unions. They owe loyalties to their old schools, universities, colleges, regiments, clubs, even political parties. Of most of us it is true that, so far from being individuals having to choose between stark alternatives like the 'common good' or 'our own individual interest' we owe loyalties to the various groupings to which we belong, pigeon fanciers, Rotarians, Women's Institutes, Mothers' Unions, and to each of these we often subordinate our own interests and sometimes prefer them, or choose the interests of one group to whom we owe loyalty rather than another. So let us beware of dichotomies, over-simplifications, ideologies, absolute and subordinate loyalties. Diversity in unity and unity in diversity are at once the glory and the characteristic of our own and all other civilised and free societies. To seek to turn modern political controversy into a battle between the material interest of the individual and the state, or between one class and another, or between 'welfare' and 'greed' is an over-simplification too common in practice, and, if translated into action, may be capable of destructive and disastrous results.

IV

The Monarchy

ANY DISCUSSION of our traditional constitution must begin with some account of our hereditary headship of state and the role of the occupant of this position. This is no formal obeisance to an outworn institution nor a perfunctory courtesy to a much-loved Sovereign Lady or her family. All countries need a head of state, and in ours the influence of the Monarch and the monarchy is all-pervasive even where it is least easily discerned, and not less because it is no longer associated with personal rule.

I wish to make it clear at the outset that, however trite or universally acceptable the observation may sound, the position of the Monarch is the one element in our Constitution in which I would advocate no formal change whatever, either in its powers or in the part it plays generally in society. I say 'formal change' because all institutions evolve with the societies in which they are placed and the monarchy is no exception to this. I was born in the reign of Edward VII, and have lived successively in the reigns of George V, Edward VIII, George VI, and the present Queen. The tradition has been continuous, but it is idle to deny that there have been changes not only in personality and style, but still more in external circumstances such as the political climate of the times, the sequence and influence of international events, the alternation of peace and war, and the social climate and structure of successive generations. Even formal changes in title have been effected in these evolutionary processes. No longer, after the loss of empire, is the Sovereign referred to as Emperor or Empress. The title of Head of the Commonwealth is entirely new, and, despite our entry into the European Community, not without contemporary political significance. However, since our discussion is primarily about our domestic arrangements and not our international role, this last point may be safely ignored.

At home the institution and the personality of the Sovereign remain all-pervasive and of permanent value. As has already been pointed out, it is an immense advantage that, in contrast to the United States, the offices of head of state and head of government are now permanently separated from one another. This automatically removes the desperate conflicts of interest and loyalties experienced in those countries which have an elective and executive President, whether himself the head of government, as in the United States, or rivalled by and often at odds with, a Prime Minister in the legislature, as in the Fifth French Republic. Still greater, of course, is the contrast to be marked in those countries where a strutting and bemedalled figure, even if elected, claims at once to exercise more or less unbridled power, and at the same time to act as the apex and focus of political loyalty to the state and the symbol of national tradition, continuity, patriotism, and pride. An equally striking contrast may be drawn between our own institution and the other kind of republican presidency where a wholly uncontentious, but usually decrepit and superannuated nonentity is selected or elected as nominal head of state precisely because he or she is harmless and innocuous, and then has to cope from time to time with the political crises attendant on a so-called 'hung parliament'. For myself, I am content to believe that our own possession of a King or Queen, necessarily varying in age and experience with the years, but inheriting the throne on succession, consecrated by a religious ceremony at a Coronation service of venerable if sometimes obscure traditions, supported by a varied and vigorous family and surrounded by a hereditary aristocracy is a treasure of immense value, especially when accompanied and embellished by occasional pageantry and ceremonial deriving from long tradition. That a monarch's duties are real and occasionally involve courage and leadership of no mean order was demonstrated by King Juan Carlos of Spain when confronted by an attempted and violent military coup, and by the histories of the Royal Families of Scandinavia and the Netherlands during the last war. Those who, in one capacity or another, have served in public offices which bring them close to the throne or have otherwise brought them into contact with Royalty, though honourably debarred from writing or speaking of their experiences, can, I think, almost without exception, testify to the immense dedication to duty and diplomacy which all members of the Royal circle bring to their respective public and private activities, as well as to the conscientious application with which monarchs in successive reigns have chosen to inform themselves about public affairs in order to enable them to perform those continuing activities described in his own day by Walter Bagehot. One anecdote, however, I think I may permit myself without indiscretion. At a reception in Downing Street to celebrate the seventieth birthday of Lord Thorneycroft I had a conversation with the late Lord Mountbatten. It was in fact the last conversation we ever held with one another before his execrable assassination by the IRA. In it he referred in the warmest terms to our present Queen, in whose circle, of course, he moved quite freely. 'And do you realise,' he said by way of conclusion 'that she is the most experienced head of state in the world?' At the time, this observation was not quite true, since the late Emperor of Japan (to name only one) was still on his throne. But long since then, it has become the fact, and, perhaps, no single consideration can better illustrate the practical advantage of having a hereditary head of state, who, like Elizabeth I, came to the throne at the age of twenty-five and continued in office at least until her sixties. I am myself wholly persuaded that of all our institutions, this is one with which I would be least inclined to meddle.

V

Executive and Legislature

FROM THE NORMAN CONQUEST ONWARDS, England was equipped with an unusually powerful, though not unlimited, central executive, at first apparently securely resting on its hereditary monarchy, endowed with an assured income derived from feudal dues, inherited possessions and various assorted prerogatives and patronage. Let us not deride the importance of this asset which has been the cause of many of the triumphs and successes of our history. In a much altered form, it is with us still, and in any changes we make, we should be careful to retain both its centrality and its strength.

But, from about the end of the fifteenth century, until the Glorious Revolution put an end to that flaw, the inherent strength of the executive under the Monarch was progressively weakened by the chronic and increasing insufficiency of the royal revenues to meet more than a relatively small proportion of the legitimate requirements of government, even in times of peace. Whether this chronic impecuniosity was partly the cause of our series, ultimately unsuccessful, of wars of aggression against France in the fourteenth and fifteenth centuries may be open to question. Probably it was. But it certainly explains the repeated devices of Henry VII to raise revenue, by various forms of extortion and forced loans and his alleged parsimony in spending what he raised. Henry VIII chose to supplement his income by despoiling the monasteries and selling their estates to the ancestors of the Whig aristocracy. The same cause also was at work in Elizabeth I's support of the various plundering and colonising expeditions of Drake and Raleigh in the new world. When these came to an end, the stage was set for the long struggle between the Crown and Parliament, since increased taxation proved the only other, and, in fact, the only legitimate source of raising revenue. This struggle filled the whole of the next century until it culminated in the succession of William III and the foundation of the Bank of England and the national debt. It ended with the final victory of Parliament over the Crown, and, gradually, owing to the necessity to obtain a majority in the House of Commons, the cabinet system took over both the prerogatives of the Crown and the power of the central executive, at first through an adroit use of patronage and corruption, and later from the first Reform Bill onwards, as of right. By now Income Tax and VAT, voted by an increasingly docile House of Commons, have taken over from Ship Money and the sale of offices of profit under the Crown. Even now, however, the taxation system needs to be supplemented by the Public Sector Borrowing Requirement.

But the enlargement of the franchise, and the system of voting which accompanied it, gradually altered the balance of power within parliament itself. The process has been more continuous than one might suppose. Almost one hundred and fifty years ago, Disraeli made his character Sidonia remark to Coningsby: 'England is governed by Downing Street; once it was governed by Alfred and Elizabeth'. The process by which parliament became in so many ways subordinate to and controlled by the executive was not invented in the twentieth century, as is suggested in so much twentieth-century literature about the Constitution. Still less is it the product of Mrs Thatcher's tenancy of the office of Prime Minister. A strong executive with a coherent policy of controlling the public has been a feature of our political life from the first. The process has been continuous and progressive. A generation after the publication of Coningsby, Gilbert and Sullivan were putting into the mouth of Private Willis, 'on sentry go to chase monotony', the immortal words:

> When in that House MPs divide
> If they've a brain and cerebellum too
> They've got to leave that brain outside
> And vote just as their leaders tell 'em to.

Private Willis, it will be remembered, was 'an intellectual chap', and drew the correct moral from this observation:

> But then, the prospect of a lot
> Of dull MPs in close proximity
> All thinking for themselves is what
> No man can face with equanimity.

In other words, the triumph of parliament in 1688 and the Hanoverian succession in 1714 transferred the powers of the executive, which had existed and developed continuously from the first, to a committee of members of parliament checked by an officer holding the office of First Lord of The Treasury, but known popularly, first as 'The Minister' and then as 'The Prime Minister'. It did not alter the powers or the advantages of a strong and coherent executive. It simply made the executive responsible to parliament, and ultimately to the electorate, now exercising almost universal adult suffrage. What has happened since is a gradual and progressive evolution as the result of events which occurred about three hundred years ago. Recent developments have only accentuated the tendency already noted by

Disraeli and the authors of the Savoy operettas, but have not unfolded in a manner false to the inherent dynamic of a Constitution which we have inherited from the past. In criticising its present condition we should not deny that it contains much that requires careful preservation. Recent changes have been brought about by increases in the volume and intensity of the work to which the structure has been subjected, and obviously require attention. Improvements, however, must be found only after an objective study of the institutions themselves and their interaction with one another. Perhaps the most important of these institutions is the cabinet.

VI

◆◆◆

The Cabinet

IN ALL DEVELOPED COUNTRIES not governed by an executive presidency or praesidium, executive power is wielded by a cabinet presided over by a Prime Minister. This almost universal institution was first developed in Britain. Legally, it is somewhat surprising to note, it may be doubted whether the cabinet exists. In a sense it is no more than a collection of ministers, most, but not necessarily all, of whom hold office with functions defined by law. As late as my father's time, and once, exceptionally, in my own, its meetings were summoned by a quaint document stating that 'A meeting of HIS/HER Majesty's servants will be held at (No 10 Downing Street) on (Tuesday the –st July 19–)'. The office of Prime Minister was known as such or by the similar title 'The Minister' from Walpole's time, but, until well into the nineteenth century, it was officially, and strenuously, denied that such an office existed. The earliest official reference I can find was when Disraeli signed the Treaty of Berlin with the non-existent title 'Prime Minister of England' (sic) written after his name. A *London Gazette* of 1905 contains a reference to the 'Prime Minister' as such, and from Baldwin's time onwards the Prime Minister has been given as such a place in the table of precedence. Customarily the Prime Minister is given the ancient office of

First Lord of the Treasury, which presumably dates from the time when the Lord Treasurer's office was put into Commission as too grand for a mere subject to hold. Presumably the cabinet itself ranks as an unofficial committee of the Privy Council. By custom, all members are Privy Councillors (or Counsellors as purists prefer to spell the word), and, in addition to liability under the Official Secrets Act, have to swear a Privy Council oath, apparently drafted in the sixteenth century by Henry VIII in one of his less agreeable moods. No doubt the cabinet owes its present form to the fact that Henry, with Thomas Cromwell at his right hand, designed the Privy Council as the principal organ of Tudor despotism, and made sure that only a handful of members, carefully hand-picked, were actually summoned to any particular meeting. Until the end of the reign of Queen Anne, the Sovereign actually presided and, even today, in the Old Treasury Board Room, where some cabinet committee meetings are regularly held, there is a throne at the head respectfully raised on a low dais so that the Sovereign should be able to sit at a level slightly above that of the subjects present. Until well into the twentieth century, there were no minutes, and minutes were only finally introduced owing to the difficulty experienced by cabinet ministers in remembering, and by some civil servants in discovering, what had actually been decided. Even now, when minutes are not only taken but circulated to the Hackers, Humphrey Applebys and Bernard Bottomleys of this world, they are quite unlike the minutes of any other body to which I have belonged. They are, in effect, less a description of the discussion than a brief directive to civil servants as to the action to be taken as a result of the meetings.

Nothing can better illustrate the informal character of our constitutional arrangements than the almost total absence of a strict legal basis for some of their most vital elements. In this, very real, sense, ours is indeed an unwritten Constitution.

By 1924, when my father was first a member of the cabinet, in addition to the meetings of the full cabinet, which were attended by a secretary and the government Chief Whip in the Commons, much of the business of the growing work of government was in practice carried on by a structure of standing cabinet committees covering distinct areas of policy. These, which, of course, still exist in more or less the same form, were not confined to cabinet ministers and, though chaired by a senior cabinet minister, could be attended by junior ministers and even senior civil servants representing interested departments. Although everyone was perfectly well aware of their existence and importance, their designations, functions and membership were supposed to be a deadly secret protected by the supposedly equally secret terms of the Privy Councillors' oath.

Since my father's day a new development has occurred. Though the regular committees still carry out their ever increasing load of regular work and remain the main instruments for carrying out the day-to-day business of cabinet government, a growing practice has been developed of ad hoc meetings of varying composition and numbers, often comprising a very small number of ministers with the Prime Minister usually in the chair, but occasionally, like the group of ministers who met at intervals throughout the Suez crisis following on the nationalisation of the Canal, larger bodies of fluctuating membership not confined to the cabinet or even to ministers. Probably, under cabinet government, such informal gatherings have always taken place. But, at least since Suez, they have proliferated almost indefinitely and have become a regular and important, if contentious, instrument of government policy. From the point of view of day-to-day management these somewhat amorphous floating bodies have considerable practical advantages. They have helped full meetings of the cabinet itself to be reduced from two to one a week despite the rising volume of business. They enable differences between ministers to be settled more privately, and, in the case of the 'Star Chamber' meetings prior to the settlement of expenditure plans, more efficiently, than before. Without something like them it is doubtful whether cabinet government could continue to carry out the full and increasing load of business which falls on its shoulders. Nevertheless the existence of this multifarious conglomeration of informal bodies does reduce the sense of collegiality between ministers without which no government can hold together, and, quite inevitably, they enhance the power of the Prime Ministerial office. They are also partly instrumental in the use, or abuse, of the lobby system as a means of 'leaking' information or canvassing opinions. This is not confined to the Press Office at Downing Street, but, in my view, has been used as a device by other ministers as well. All this, together with the growing power of the media, particularly television, fuels speculation that we may be moving towards a presidential system of government and away from the collegiality of cabinet. Another development is the growing practice of cabinet ministers of keeping private diaries, or, after retirement, publishing memoirs containing passages derogatory of former colleagues and unprotected by the traditional licence granted to ministers in a resignation statement to parliament. The judgement of the late Lord Widgery supporting the publication of the Crossman diaries, whilst supportive of judicial independence of politics and politicians, did nothing to restrain this tendency.

One can, however, overstate the case. It is true that a number of factors, some of which remain to be discussed, have given colour to the suggestion that so far from being controlled by parliament, the cabinet through the Whips is controlling the House of Commons, and that the Prime Minister, by the powers of patronage in the appointment and requiring the resignation of ministers, controls the cabinet. Nevertheless, despite the strain from the growing complexity and volume of work, cabinet government is still alive and kicking, and the powers of the House of Commons over ministers and even Prime Ministers remain far from negligible. Whatever other moral may be drawn from the somewhat unedifying episode of the departure from office of Mrs Thatcher on the eve of the so-called Gulf War, the events of 1990 establish beyond doubt that, in the last resort, individual members of cabinet, when backed by a substantial minority on the backbenches, are still firmly in control of the Ship of State. Even the more troubling aspects of the case are less unedifying than the circumstances surrounding the departure of Richard Nixon by the disclosure of the tapes and the threat of impeachment. It may be that cabinet government is the better system after all.

VII

———— ◆◆ ————

Party and the Party System

LEGALLY, like the cabinet itself and its subordinate committees and structures, the existence, number, identity and designation of parties form no part of our Constitution. But, if it is to be understood at all, it is absolutely unavoidable that some discussion of the nature and machinery of the party and party system should take place at this stage of the argument. Party lies at the hinge of procedure in both Houses of Parliament. Party determines the composition of the House of Commons, and, to a large extent, that of the Lords. Party lies at the root of cabinet government in all parliamentary democracies. It is necessary to add that in single party states party is an essential tool of tyranny.

It is a paradox, as will be shown, but no coincidence, that, in countries based on the British tradition, the number of parties available for public choice has always tended to gravitate towards the number of two, with any additional parties operating mainly on the fringe. This is not one of the laws of nature. In many other countries, particularly those in the European parliamentary tradition, a multi-party system is much more common. Consistently with this, in countries following the British tradition of the two parties, it is more common than not for each of the two parties to win election battles outright, whilst the rule under the other pattern is for the result of elections to end inconclusively with no party obtaining an absolute majority, except, of course, in those cases like the US Presidency where the election is to a specific office, which can only be held by a single person. Since much current political controversy revolves round these differences, it is worth while considering their causes and whether they represent an advantage or otherwise for the effective operation of a parliamentary government.

Long before the advent of democracy, our own method of voting consisted of a system in which there was only one ballot, and in which the successful candidate or candidates (usually one or two in number), irrespective of whether they commanded an absolute majority, succeeded in getting the largest number of votes. No doubt, from time to time, independent members or members belonging to minority groupings would emerge successfully from such a contest. But such cases, however, have always been the exception rather than the rule. Under other systems, where there are strong and distinct nationalist, religious or linguistic minorities at work in a heterogeneous community, third forces continually emerge and exercise continuous influence more or less in proportion to the relative strength of their adherents. This was true in Ireland in 1914. But over three hundred years, and given the system I have described both before and after the emergence of democracy, the Anglo-Saxon tradition has tended to conform to a two-party pattern, whether the parties were labelled Court and Country, Whig and Tory, Liberal and Conservative, Conservative and Labour or, as in the United States, Republicans and Democrats, in Australia Liberal and Labour or, as in Canada, New Zealand, and South Africa before the death of Smuts, by other and differing designations. Given other systems of voting, it is equally noticeable that the results of

34

elections tend to result in the emergence of many party groupings.

The reason is obvious. In the absence of coherent ethnic, religious or linguistic minorities, as in India, or Northern Ireland, party divisions do not represent static groups of opinion entitled by reason of their inherent cohesion to proportionate representation in the legislature. On the contrary, the demarcations of the main party divisions and subdivisions, whether in multi-party situations or two-party situations, are caused by the system of voting in operation at the time, and not by distinct and static groups of voters each representing a minority entitled to an equal chance of success. Thus, it is not sensible to ask whether, except in the particular cases I have described, particular systems are 'fair' to the different parties. Given a relatively homogeneous population, representing a wide and continuously shifting spectrum of opinion and a wide variation of interest, the question of the 'fairness' of a system is meaningless until it is grasped that the continuity and lines of demarcation between the party groups are brought about by the nature of the system of voting and do not represent separate and distinct groupings which exist independently of it. The real question to answer is pragmatic. What system of voting best serves the national interest, and whether and to what extent, an existing system should be changed with a view to producing better results.

There are, of course, plenty of suggested alternatives to choose from. There is our own, 'first past the post' system. There is the system of 'party lists', with vast, multi-member constituencies. There is voting in one ballot in order of preference or by single transferable vote. There is voting by second and subsequent ballots to give in the end an absolute majority to one surviving candidate or party. There are many others. Given that there can be combinations and

35

variations of these different options, there are probably not less than twenty possible systems of which a considerable number have been tried, with varying results in different places. Moreover, it is perfectly possible to argue that the choice of system may depend on the purpose for which the election is designed. Are we engaged in the choice of a single individual for a designated office, say a President or a Mayor? Are we electing a national legislative assembly, or a local council which combines executive and legal powers? Is the assembly to be governed by an executive holding separate offices but a common party loyalty as in a cabinet, or, as is common in organs of local government, by committees or plenary meetings composed of members of different affiliations under the general authority of plenary sessions deciding or ruling by majority voting? Is the assembly itself sovereign in its own field, or does it perform subordinate functions delegated by general legislation or central government? There is plenty of room for differing opinions in the several cases, and it is difficult to argue in general terms that the system which suits one type of election is best for the others. For most cases, there may well be a balance of advantage easily discerned. In others, there will doubtless emerge disadvantages to be avoided at almost any cost. In some of the opinions I advance, I may sound a little more than dogmatic. But I shall seek to remedy this as the argument proceeds.

Once it is accepted that, in the absence of distinct communities within the nation each entitled to representation in an elected institution and equality in status if not in numbers, the question to be asked is what system of voting in what pattern of constituencies best serves the public interest, and not what system, given universal suffrage, is in the abstract 'fair' in any democracy. On this assumption certain generalities begin to emerge.

The first of these is that, given a legislature to which an executive is to be responsible, composed of ministers under a Prime Minister forming a cabinet, multiplicity of parties is not in general desirable, and not in essence necessarily democratic. I do not know how many separate administrations have been formed in Italy since the war. At the time of writing, I believe that the total is not much less than fifty, and I believe that their average life has not been much more than nine months. Contrast that with the British model. Here most administrations command an absolute majority in the legislature even if not amongst the electorate and more often than not the same majority remains in office for at least two terms. Given this effect, which appears predictable, the advantage of a two-party system can be clearly discerned. Constant changes of government responsible to a legislature with no discernible majority prevent any real continuity of policy and bear little relation to popular wishes. Moreover, such policies as do emerge from cabinets can in the nature of things have little to do with any of the party manifestos preceding the election, and, therefore, little to do with anything for which any of the electorate have consciously voted. In the nature of things, they are nothing but cobbled compromises made up in the legendary smoke-filled rooms, and the evil is compounded where, as is common in such cases, the legislature is elected for a fixed term and cannot, or cannot easily, be dissolved in the case of inability to agree. In addition, the head of state (in Italy the President) is inevitably drawn into the negotiation for cabinet formation, and from time to time must therefore inevitably become the object of controversy either for what he has done in helping to create the ephemeral administration which emerges from the bargaining process or, worse still, for what he has failed to accomplish during the periods of interregnum when no credible government at all has remained in office for any respectable length of time.

One must also dismiss as illusion the widespread belief that any of the proposed alternatives favours either moderate parties or moderation in policy. As often as not, it is the extremists who gain a foothold and many even possess the balance of power. It was one or other of the variant alternatives which explains the existence, even during the cold war, of powerful Communist or Trotskyite groups in some of the parliaments of Western Europe. The battle is not always for the moderate centre. Sinn Fein, which openly supports the IRA, has secured a parliamentary foothold in Northern Ireland, and, in that unhappy province extreme forms of sectarianism can flourish even among the less overtly sectarian groups from both communities. Any form of proportionality in voting may assist such developments. The same tendency to favour extremism has also in recent years appeared in beleaguered Israel where the balance of power is held by extremist religious minorities. It is even arguable that the end of the Weimar Republic which led to the rise of Adolf Hitler was the result of the impeccably liberal system of voting under that regime. Under our present system of voting it is the moderate wing of each party which has tended to predominate. While it must have been very discouraging to Liberals to have maintained a separate existence for so many years without ever once enjoying a spell of office outside local government, it is difficult to see that any public disadvantage has occurred, and it is at least arguable that their disappointment is as much due to a healthy distrust in the minds of electors of their faulty analysis of the rival advantages of differing voting systems as to any excessive ration of original sin inherent in either or both of the two major parties. At various times members of the Conservative and Labour parties (not least Winston Churchill himself), have toyed with the idea of, or even actively

proclaimed their support for, different and usually unspeci-
fied, variations on the theme of electoral reform. So far as
I am concerned, the more I reflect upon the subject, the
more I prefer the status quo. Our system of single member
constituencies and first past the post voting has given us
the strong and coherent executives that every free country
requires. It has served and continues to serve us well, better,
I believe, than any other. So far as the House of Commons
is concerned, I hope it may continue to be the rule, and
I am greatly depressed when I read of otherwise serious
characters propounding the alleged advantages of a so-
called 'hung parliament'. A 'hung parliament' is a borrowed
Americanism derived from a 'hung jury'. A 'hung jury' is a
jury which cannot make up its mind. Neither juries nor
parliaments which cannot make up their minds are of much
value to man or beast. For juries at least, a hung jury may
lead to a new trial. But for parliaments, time and tide wait
for no man. An electorate which has a limited choice of
possible alternative parties each of which has a chance of
winning is the electorate which wields the greatest authority
in determining the result.

VIII

The House of Commons

'ALL POWER resides in the House of Commons,' said my friend, colleague and mentor, Oliver Poole, more than thirty years ago. 'And,' he added percipiently, 'all leaks derive from the top and originate in the lobby.' He meant lobby briefing. Both propositions remain true today. It may well be that Prime Ministers have a higher profile nowadays, but only so long as they maintain the loyalty of senior colleagues. It may well be that, through the Whips and the threat of dissolution, the cabinet can exercise tighter control in the division lobbies on particular issues and in passing guillotine motions on particular measures. But cabinet ministers who sit in the Commons owe their original appointment to their power to influence the House. Once lose this, they soon lose office. Sometimes their potential departure is adumbrated by depreciatory remarks 'from sources close to the Prime Minister' and attributed to 'our political correspondent'. We talk about the 'collegiality of the cabinet' and 'cabinet responsibility'. Some of us point to the potential dangers, always present because inherent in our Constitution, of elective dictatorship or the increasingly 'presidential' role of the Prime Minister. Obviously the existence of a hereditary head of state and an influential though never decisive second chamber limit the danger of a dictatorial majority in the Commons dominating a cowed and impatient opposition. But the House of Commons, as at present elected, normally guided by an absolute majority of one party and challenged by well organised opposition, with one party and a 'shadow cabinet' normally on the front opposition bench, remains the real source of political power and the main focus of political debate. We may be amused at the intrigues of Sir Humphrey Appleby or James Hacker in *Yes Minister* or *Yes Prime Minister*. Like all good caricatures this satire contains and exposes some important elements of truth. For a time, the back benches, particularly when the majority is small, may be restrained by threats of dissolution if they rebel. But in the long run, it is the back benches who have the last word. I first became aware of this at the outset of my father's career in 1922 when the 'Carlton Club meeting' brought down the Lloyd George coalition and after the General Election which followed ushered in the Bonar Law government. In those days all the main organs of a soberer press than we have today published long extracts from the speeches in parliament of the previous day. There were few 'parliamentary sketch writers', no real radio reports and, of course, no television coverage. The House of Lords, rightly chastened by the terrifying experiences of 1909 and 1911, had already ceased to challenge the Commons, and were still unimproved by the creation of life peers, the introduction of leave of absence or the right of disclaimer.

This does not mean that nothing has changed in my lifetime, nor that all changes have been for the better. I doubt, for instance, whether the introduction of select committees shadowing particular departments, an import from the USA, has been a boon rather than a bore, and even, at times, an irrelevant diversion.

The real genius of the House of Commons rests on the

floor of the House and not on the committee floor whether on standing or select committees. The contrast may readily be seen by anyone who listens for even five minutes to the extraordinarily arid debates in the Senate and House of Representatives in Congress. The difference, of course, lies in the presence of ministers on the floor of the House of Commons where they can speak, or be questioned, slay or be slain, and where, in any high-profile debate, the most intense drama occurs.

The real, and dominating, change which has been going on in parliament since Victorian times is the immense and exponential increase in the volume of work and in particular of legislation for which parliament has, directly or indirectly, become responsible.

In Victorian days, Gladstone as Chancellor of the Exchequer was able to describe Income Tax, now surely the flagship of direct taxation, as a 'sleeping giant'. The giant soon awoke and has been increasingly active ever since. The whole Lloyd George Budget of 1909 which caused such a rumpus at the time, was for a total of £150 million, golden sovereigns no doubt, but still only £150 million. In the inter-war period, the typical budget, paper pounds except between Churchill's period of office as Chancellor and 1931, was about £800 million rising to £1000 million. Public expenditure now currently runs at about £200,000 million of our present currency.

Another good yardstick is the volume of legislation. The radical government of 1911 passed little more than 450 pages of public general statutes. Apart from the exceptional, but for this purpose irrelevant, year of 1925, a typical session's work between the wars was 1000 pages plus a good number of pieces of secondary legislation, roundly condemned by Lord Hewart in *The New Despotism*. There are very few years in which contemporary governments, Conservative or Labour, pass much less than 3000 pages of primary and 10,000 pages of secondary, legislation and recent years have yielded even more abundant harvests. It is impossible for institutions to digest changes on a scale and of a volume of this sort without producing changes in their structure and character, and these in turn prove not merely changes of scale and degree, but changes in kind.

Some of these changes are good. The absurd length of the speeches indulged in by the Victorians even, for instance, Disraeli as a backbencher, is rightly forgotten. In the famous Don Pacifico debate Lord Palmerston rose to address the House whilst the sun was setting on a summer evening. By the time he reached his peroration of 'Civis Britannicus sum', the sun was rising across the Thames (which runs north and south at Westminster), the following morning.

That this sort of turgid oratory, confined now to dictators, is no longer tolerated in either House is wholly to the good. But despite the shorter speeches, the right of speech at all has necessarily been curtailed. Private members Bills are, perhaps rightly, largely driven off the agenda. The closure, the 'kangaroo' (the Speaker's power to pass over amendments) and the 'guillotine', at first introduced hesitantly by Gladstone as one of the 'resources of civilisation' called out against Irish obstruction, are now part of everyday parliamentary usage. Incidentally, and a plus, the reduction of the total numbers of members as the result of the loss of the Southern Irish constituencies and the university seats has made the House of Commons a much less unwieldy body, despite the loss of some colourful characters of both classes. Without Gladstone's 'resources of civilisation', almost universally thought disastrous in their time, and the reduction in numbers, I doubt whether any modern government could cope with its increased business.

Not all the changes, however, have been beneficial. As

a tool of investigation, apart from the already existing Accounts and Expenditure Committees, select committees had, I thought, totally discredited themselves at the time of the so-called Marconi scandal of 1914, and I deplore their reintroduction as watchdogs, shadowing departments. Tribunals of enquiry appointed under the Act of 1921 to investigate alleged scandals are much better, and parliament has at its command a vast range of instruments of enquiry to suit a wide range of general and particular investigations. As I have already explained, I distrust imports or reimports from America, not from any want of admiration for my mother's country, but because of the essentially different genius and structure of their Constitution. In the House of Commons, ministers can be questioned on the floor, or bearded in the tearoom or smoking room. In Congress they have to be grilled upstairs by a committee.

However, the committees of the Commons are probably the least unfavourable developments. Unavoidable, probably, is the undue pressure on time, which is partly due to the over-centralised nature of our arrangements. Unavoidable too are the intrusion and requirements of radio and television. But other developments have not been necessary. One is Prime Minister's Question Time (another import from across the Atlantic, in imitation of the Presidential press conferences) and the sad deterioration in the tone and spirit of debate. One should never, of course, pretend that political controversy can ever be devoid of rancour, nor that the House of Commons has ever been universally noted for decorous and serene behaviour. None the less, without naming names, behaviour has deteriorated badly since the war with verbal abuse, excessive party prejudice and bogus and time-wasting points of order making the conduct of civilised debate in the Commons difficult, and, at times, impossible.

When I was first elected to the House of Commons,

Prime Minister's question time virtually did not exist. I say 'virtually' because, with difficulty, it was just possible to ask a Prime Minister a question, related not to general policy but to the strict conduct of the Prime Ministerial office. Such questions were usually one in number on any given day, and since they were always numbered forty-five and therefore seldom, if ever, reached for oral answer, they seldom attracted much notice.

Some time between 1950 when I left the Commons on inheriting my father's title and my return, after disclaiming my hereditary title at the end of 1963, the bi-weekly bull fights held at 3.15 p.m. on Tuesdays and Thursdays had already begun. Since then they have flourished like the green bay tree. With the advent of the so-called 'open question' and the concentration by radio and TV on these bi-weekly exhibitions they have become a regular display of bad manners and noisy exchange.

The expression 'the open question' may need some further explanation. Since its invention, virtually all questions listed for oral answer on Tuesdays and Thursdays, and given a secure place in the last quarter of an hour reserved for question time, take the same form and use the same words. 'To ask the Prime Minister whether he/she will list his/her engagements on (the date for which the question is listed).' It is impossible to say the question is out of order, and it is invariably answered in a tedious list of boring engagements. It would make no difference whatever were it not. The point of the open question is that it is generally accepted that almost any supplementary question is in order. 'Can my right honourable friend (or 'the right honourable gentleman or lady') not find time to consider the appalling case of my constituent Mrs Smith, who . . .'. Or 'can he/she give careful consideration to the serious situation now developing in Ruritania (or the economy, or whatever else the questioner may wish to ask)'. The result is a farce, lowering to the whole dignity of debate and the atmosphere of calm and objective discussion which should characterise public controversy. The farce is compounded by two factors. Prime Ministers of either political persuasion usually revel in the fray and employ expert civil servants and colleagues to prepare themselves for it at the expense of their more serious duties. They usually pride themselves that they conduct themselves skilfully. Worse still, they usually do. The second factor is that by convention, after the first supplementary question has been called the Leader of the Opposition is privileged to catch the Speaker's eye – and the farce develops into a bull fight with the Leader of the Opposition seeking to play the part of the matador, and various would-be toreadors seeking to tire the bull with numerous undignified diversions, and the aficionados shouting encouragement or the reverse from the ringside. No doubt as a rule the whole lamentable exhibition is reasonably amusing entertainment. But the damage done to the House of Commons and to the dignity of public life will, I believe, be enormous, lasting and even irreparable, particularly as the whole encounter makes admirable viewing and listening entertainment on TV and radio. There are already signs of a new step downhill in the rake's progress. There is already a substantial demand that we should degrade the standards of the Courts of Law by televising a few selected episodes from sensational but equally selected trials. If television were only a sort of window through which a wider number of people could watch what actually goes on in public at present, there could be no possible objection. It might even be an advantage. But television in its essence is not just a window. It is a catalyst, altering the form and context of what is going on, usually for the worse, but also sometimes, it must be conceded, for the better. In the Commons it is not merely TV and radio which corrupt. It is the whole ethos of Prime Minister's questions as they have developed. Since this has coincided with a general decline in parliamentary standards in the Commons, the evil is compounded. My own opinion is that a general review is overdue in which the whole question of procedure in the House of Commons should be examined. On the agenda should be a great deal more than Prime Minister's questions. The whole question of the preparation, presentation and discussion of Bills, should be considered, the time available for general debates, the methods for promoting private members' bills, the use to be made of timetable motions, and the extent to which the Speaker's office should be advised and administered.

A final question remains, which I reserve for further consideration. In view of my analysis, is it possible that the House of Commons is not only too large, but *much* too large? If so, and if the numbers had to be reduced, how could the interests of constituents and constituencies be adequately represented?

IX

The House of Lords

No one in his right mind could ever have invented the House of Lords, with its archbishops and bishops, Lords of Appeal in Ordinary, hereditary peerages marshalled into hierarchical grades of dukes, marquesses, earls, viscounts and barons, its life peers nominated by the executive, its truncated powers, its absence of internal discipline and its liability to abolition. The case for reform seems unanswerable. Indeed, in the first of the two Parliament Acts, the Liberal government of 1911 announced its intention of replacing the House of Lords in its existing form, then predominantly hereditary, with an elected second chamber, rather pompously asserting that the question 'brooked no delay'. Instead, the House of Lords has continued to exist more or less as it was, but evolving continuously as it went along, with life peerages now its predominant element, Scottish peers admitted as of right, Irish peerages as such extinct as a means of membership, registered leave of absence admitted as a ground for non-attendance, disclaimer a permitted avenue of escape for reluctant hereditaries, and its legal powers further curtailed by the totally unnecessary Parliament Act of 1949. After eighty years of a problem which in 1911 'brooked no delay', the House still flourishes, more anomalous than ever, but probably more popular than at any time in its long history, performing an indispensable function in discussing the hugely increased volume of legislation, its debates a model of civilised and orderly argument, well publicised on television and radio, its membership eagerly sought after, and making available to parliament an otherwise untapped reservoir of talent, experience and distinction.

What is the explanation of this extraordinary paradox, at first sight so anomalous as to be indefensible? In saying in 1911 that its abolition 'brooked no delay', the Liberal government of the day made a number of wholly pardonable errors. In the first place it failed to appreciate that, in defeating the diehard element which had foolishly challenged the 1909 budget and temporarily held up the Home Rule legislation (later rendered obsolete by the Irish Treaty in 1921), the Commons had not merely won the battle, but had decisively won the war. Never again has the House of Lords set itself up as an effective Court of Appeal from the Commons or seriously challenged its monopoly of financial legislation. Its revising power, indispensable in modern conditions, may save the Commons from minor, hasty and ill-judged decisions and the parliamentary draftsman's office from errors and ambiguities, as well as providing a field for a vast array of uncontroversial improvements. The only question is not whether the second chamber does a useful job of work, but whether an elective second chamber with increased powers is not desirable in order to save our liberties from the perils of elective dictatorship. That this is not a purely academic question is clear from the fact that, at least theoretically speaking, the Labour Party is committed to abolition of the House of Lords without replacement, unless we include the redoubtable Mr Benn's populist, undemocratic but fortunately laughable alternative of a 'People's Chamber' to complement the Commons.

This brings me to the second error of the Liberal government of 1911. It failed to realise that a popular second chamber, however elected, would either mirror the party composition of the House of Commons, in which case it would be a superfluous rubber stamp, or be of a different party composition, in which case it could challenge the House of Commons as a serious rival, surely a recipe for confrontation without possibility of reconciliation. By continuing the House of Lords in a theoretically indefensible form the Liberal government had ensured its survival. It could perform useful functions as a complement to the House of Commons. It could never be a rival. Its theoretical indefensibility is the real guarantee of its continued usefulness.

The question remains whether any further reform is either necessary, desirable or even possible. I reject out of hand single chamber government based on a House of Commons elected as at present, with unlimited legislative powers, including the power of prolonging its own life. This is simply a synonym for elective dictatorship, and, of course, if the power to prolong its own life were included, one could omit the adjective 'elective'. We should, quite simply, cease to be a democracy even in theory. I will examine at a later stage the possibilities of a Constitution in these islands consisting of a chamber elected more or less on the basis of existing constituencies, with an elected second chamber based on large regions (to some extent self-governed by regional assemblies) but with certain powers reserved to the centre. Such an arrangement could partake of some, though not necessarily all, the characteristics of a true federation. There are arguments for and against this development. It would be necessary to formulate the place which existing local authorities, based on boroughs, districts and counties, could take under such a regime. It would also be necessary to integrate the whole pattern into the international or supra-national institutions of the European Community and the European Convention on Human Rights. At first sight the total package would seem to present a somewhat daunting image of an unduly complicated structure of government, ranging from the parish pump through district and county councils, regional assemblies and parliament up to Community Council of Ministers, Parliament and Commission. However, such speculation cannot be rejected out of hand. A second chamber elected on a regional basis on a different system of voting is not an impossibility, though it would present some at least of the disadvantages of rigidity and a written Constitution monitored and policed by a Supreme Court on the American model. It is not to be condemned out of hand. But it remains a pure speculation, and I personally find it doubtfully attractive.

In the meantime, there is another, and simpler, option available. When enthusiastic reformers approached Lord Melbourne with proposals for radical reform on any subject, he was apt to listen patiently and appreciatively, and then say 'Why not let it alone?' We are getting on quite well at the moment. For what it is worth, I tend to think that we have exhausted the possibilities of reforming the House of Lords by tinkering. The time for radical change may come, possibly even be forced on us, and may be not far distant. In the meantime, I tend to think we have more important things to do than to reform the existing, theoretically indefensible, but practically useful, and arguably indispensable, House of Lords.

Human institutions are of two classes, the traditional, and the contrived. The contrived must be judged by reason. The test of the traditional type is how well it works in practice and the quality and value of what it produces. By this test the House of Lords should survive.

X

Church and State

'MAN,' said Sidonia to Coningsby, 'is made to adore and
to obey. But if you give him nothing to worship, he will
fashion his own divinities, and find a chieftain in his own
passions.' The terrible history of the twentieth century,
starting with the decline of religion, indeed of religions,
into political ideologies, and of all popular, or populist
movements into tyrannies based on ideologies, is in part a
commentary on this insight of the prescient Disraeli. As
with individuals, the state must also make its own acknowledgement of the ultimate sovereignty of spiritual and moral
values or decline into self-worship, masquerading as ideology. The Constitution of the United Kingdom is based on
the sovereignty of the Queen in parliament and the rule of
law. But law itself is nothing but natural morality translated
into the enforceable. It has been relatively easy to discuss
the nature, development and contemporary value of our
secular institutions without a discussion of their relation to
absolute values. Monarchy, the Commons, the Lords and
the component parts of each are all institutions which are
essentially secular. So, too, are the cabinet, the party system,
the voting methods, the executive government, and the
relations between them. Some attempt must now be made
to discuss the more indefinite and intractable questions
associated with religion.

A decreasing number of political societies acknowledge a religion established by law and those that do are not distinguished for their moderation or liberalism. There is no religion or religious denomination established by law in the United Kingdom as a whole. Anomalously by law, the Queen, constitutionally advised, is the Supreme Governor (not the head) of the Church of England. She also appoints the Lord High Commissioner of the Church of Scotland, a body also established by law. But neither Wales nor Northern Ireland has any established Churches at all. A large volume of Halsbury's *Laws of England* is devoted to the ecclesiastical Law of the Established Church of England. On accession, the Sovereign must subscribe separate oaths for the preservation of the Established Church of England and the Presbyterian Church in Scotland. The oath also requires a profession that the Sovereign is a faithful Protestant. But any special privileges once accorded to Episcopal Churches in Scotland, Wales or Ireland have been done away with.

There we might leave this higgledy piggledy situation but for two factors. In the United Kingdom, every Sovereign takes part in a Coronation service ending in a Communion service according to the Anglican rite. In course of time this has become very much more than a denominational affair. It is a national, indeed an international, event viewed by hundreds of millions of persons not normally devout, and certainly not Anglican in their allegiance. It does not stop there. It is a solemn acknowledgement by the head of our otherwise secular state of the ultimate sovereignty of the spiritual and moral order in human affairs. I mention this because there is serious talk of 'disestablishing' the Church of England. So far as I know, there is no such talk of disestablishing the schism-ridden Presbyterian Church in Scotland. At this point I seem to sense the shade of the, in this life, not at all religious Lord Melbourne whispering in my ear: 'Why not let it alone?'

At first sight, disestablishment (whatever that might turn out to mean) of the Church of England would be a tidy and logical end to a somewhat complex constitutional anomaly. It would have very little effect on Roman Catholic, Jewish, Muslim, Hindu or other religious minorities, and even less on the not at all religious, who are at least as divided as the devout in their philosophies of life. Even to Anglicans, there might be very little visible difference in the actual choice and appointments of bishops, deans, canons, or whatever. To the inhabitants of Northern Ireland, Wales and Scotland there would be no difference at all.

Nevertheless in England there would be complicated and serious financial and practical questions. As part of the national heritage we have a whole series of incomparable purpose-built buildings in various parts of the country, St Paul's Cathedral, Westminster Abbey, Canterbury Cathedral, York Minster and many others. More importantly still from some points of view, there is the wonderful range of parish churches preserved in every city, town and almost every village, whose upkeep is maintained almost without support from the Treasury, largely at the expense of churchgoing Anglicans.

Like the Queen at her Coronation, most of us instinctively feel that there are various critical points of our lives, the birth of a new child, the entry into adult life, marriage, the death and burial of a beloved friend or relative, when even the least devout are consciously aware of an almost compulsive need for the numinous to satisfy our deepest feelings. Where else shall we go, unless we are active members of some other denomination or religion, to find what we seek but to one of the buildings provided by our ancestors where others have sought comfort over the centuries? At present they are kept in reasonably good repair and regular use by the, probably diminishing, number of their active adherents. At present they have to provide the services to almost all who seek them. Do we wish them to disappear, and would their disappearance benefit even the members of other denominations or any part of the United Kingdom outside England?

So far as I am concerned, Lord Melbourne wins the day. Even were I not a communicant of the Church of England, I would let it alone. I do not pretend that this is the final option. But I would not relish the immense complication of the issues to be discussed in parliament were a different course to be taken, and I doubt whether many of my fellow countrymen would fling their caps in the air when they discovered the various practical considerations and cost of the necessary increase in taxation.

XI

The Judiciary

OF THE TROIKA into which the powers of government have been separated since the end of the seventeenth century, the third is a judiciary independent alike of the government, and in practice and to a large extent of Parliament. We pride ourselves on the maintenance of this separation, which is universally accepted, at least in theory, in all civilised states.

Nevertheless, owing to differences in the judicial systems of different countries, methods of appointing, giving security of tenure, and of occasionally disciplining judges in cases of misconduct, vary. There are two broad views of a judge's functions. In Anglo-Saxon countries, the judge partakes of some of the functions of a referee in a sporting contest. The contention is primarily between the parties or their legal advisers. Each has to establish, or refute, certain propositions of fact or law. The judge controls the proceedings, blows his whistle in case of a foul, and, if sitting alone, decides the winner, or, if sitting with a jury, sums up the evidence and decides disputed questions of law. The parties are responsible for producing the witnesses and documents to assist their cases. The judge is not, at least primarily, an inquisitor, and the system is often called adversarial.

In most continental countries where the Code Napoléon

or its offshoots apply, a more inquisitorial system is in being. It is the function of the judge to find out the truth. It is he who is primarily responsible for asking questions of witnesses, and advocates are severely restricted in the questions they may ask. He prepares an elaborate dossier of everything, and, unlike the shorthand transcripts of our adversarial trials, this dossier forms the court record of the case.

Partly as a result of this difference of outlook, the nature of the judicial office differs between the two systems. In Anglo-Saxon countries, we appoint judges from the ranks of successful practising lawyers, and they tend, therefore, on appointment to be in early middle age. The advantage of this system is that we tend to get judges who know the ropes. The weakness is that, unless precautions are taken to prevent it, we may appoint judges to a position of secure tenure who, for one reason or another, are temperamentally unsuited to judicial work.

In the continental system, on the other hand, judges are a separate profession from practitioners. They leave law school in their twenties to become judges, and thereafter rise, more or less according to ability, until the end of their career. They are part of the civil service and acquire experience as their career advances. They have security of tenure, but no experience of advocacy.

In England the appointment of judges lies of course with the Sovereign but primarily with the Lord Chancellor who is responsible to parliament, except in the highest offices where the power of advising the Sovereign theoretically lies with the Prime Minister, with the Lord Chancellor having a strong influence on the choice. All methods of appointment can be criticised, but I am myself satisfied that our own works well and is certainly far superior to the American system where some judges are elected by popular vote, and others may be appointed only after a cruel, and often

politically motivated, scrutiny by a senate committee. Anyone who saw on television the treatment of Judge Borg
when he was nominated by the President to the Supreme
Court would shudder to see such a procedure adopted here,
and the more recent experience of Judge Thomas provoked
even louder cries of outrage even in the United States.

Nor is there much advantage in the introduction of a
Ministry of Justice. Responsibility for prisons and penal
treatment (with the Home Office at present), prosecutions
(with the Attorney General aided by the Director of
Public Prosecutions) and court administration (with the
Lord Chancellor) are really incompatible functions and
should be exercised by different ministers separately
responsible to parliament, with the Lord Chancellor firmly
screwed to the Woolsack, and therefore in the House
of Lords and so immune from day-to-day Commons
questioning. I am certain that if ever a Lord Chancellor
strayed beyond the strict limits of impartiality in his
patronage or disciplinary powers, he would be found out
in a matter of weeks, if not days, and his tenure of office
be brought compulsorily to an end.

So far, this is, I believe, the most satisfactory system
which could be devised. But there are features which, to be
frank, I do not like. Until recently, when it was taken over
by the Lord Chancellor, there was no satisfactory responsibility for the magistrates' courts which are given the duty
of trying over 95 per cent of the crime in England and
Wales, as well as dealing with much of the family law work.
In my view the English courts should be the responsibility
of the Lord Chancellor's office, subject to one qualification
which is that much court administration is properly judicial
business in which no minister should interfere. Otherwise,
subject to local consultation, the location and management
of courts, and the career structure and appointment of staff

should be within the remit of the Circuit administration.

Secondly, responsibility for criminal evidence and procedure should not be left, as now, with the Home Secretary. Again and again, errors of judgement have been made partly as the result of popular and populist pressure and partly from the inexperience in this field of ministers and civil servants. I would go further than this, and even believe that the serious miscarriages of justice which have taken place in some notorious cases in recent times have very largely been due to the artificiality, rigidity and obsolete origin of some of the rules in this field especially in the areas of evidence and procedure. It is these which have led to the wholly unacceptable tendency in some police circles to cut corners in methods of obtaining confessions or the preparation of other evidence. The result has been that convictions have been overturned as unsafe or unsatisfactory years after sentence has been pronounced and in some cases served and previous appeals rejected. Much of this has unjustly rubbed off on the judiciary who can, after all, only decide cases on the evidence which is put before them. If this has been tampered with at source, a wrong decision is inevitable until new material is brought to light to disclose the true facts of the case. Such happenings have other undesirable side effects. As a result of losing confidence in the system, many juries acquit when they ought to have convicted, and, though this is less heinous than the converse, it must be remembered that an acquittal of a guilty man when a proper verdict would have been a conviction is just as much, though less scandalous, a miscarriage of justice as the converse case. That this is a serious matter can be seen from the following fact. Of contested cases in indictable crime, the odds are now slightly more in favour of an acquittal than of a conviction. Even twenty years ago this was not so. This must be unsatisfactory, since it can only be explained on one (or both) of two assumptions. Either we are subjecting a number of persons who ought never to have been tried to a criminal prosecution, or in a number of cases where there ought to have been a conviction, juries have acquitted.

It must not be supposed that the strains on our system are purely of a structural character. Despite exponential increases in the number of judges, whole and part time, the number of courts available, and of the practising profession in both its branches, there has been a vast expansion in the volume of court business to be transacted. Indictable crime has been increasing since the war at a rate of approximately ten per cent a year at compound interest. As the result of the increased number of broken marriages, family legal business, which may continue long after a decree of dissolution has been pronounced, has also increased enormously. Building and construction litigation and personal injury cases have risen. A new branch of practice has come into being as the result of the development of judicial review. Whenever a natural or man-made disaster occurs, there are immediate demands for an enquiry, often enough 'a judicial enquiry chaired by a High Court judge'. Although I find it difficult to agree with all he said, it is hardly to be wondered that, at a recent Mansion House dinner, the Lord Chief Justice declared that the judicial system was approaching crisis. My own view is that the well-known laws of supply and demand, the only man-made laws universally obeyed, will ultimately reach equilibrium. But, before that time comes, there will be difficult days for those who have to administer justice. The pool of talent from which good judges can be appointed is limited by the size of the entry into the profession occurring about ten or twenty years before the date when appointments have to be made, and the one solution which is not acceptable is to lower the standards against which permanent appointments are considered.

There is a further area in which reform is needed. The Act of Settlement, which requires the resolution of each House of Parliament before a judge is removed, has worked well for over three hundred years. It is otherwise with the lower judiciary. It is well enough for the lay magistracy to be subject to the discretionary jurisdiction of the Lord Chancellor. But it is otherwise with professional judges in the lower ranks. There exist in almost every Commonwealth jurisdiction (including Scotland) adequate procedures for a fair trial of subordinate judges accused of incapacity or misbehaviour. It is high time a similar procedure, subject to ultimate accountability to parliament, were introduced into England and Wales.

XII

◆◆◆

The Armed Forces

IN BRITAIN, it is not possible in the context of the Constitution to write about defence and the defence forces without seeming complacent. Prior to James II's 'abdication' the possession by the Crown of a standing army (the Royal Navy never caused the same trouble, save for the financial hiccup about Ship Money) was considered to be, and was, a threat to liberty, and for about a hundred years after his fall constitutional writers so regarded it. The Annual Army Act (as it used to be called) was the sovereign remedy which we owe to the Glorious Revolution. Countries where Common Law does not hold sway have not been so fortunate. Neither the Iberian Peninsula nor the former colonies of Spain and Portugal in South America and the Caribbean have been immune from military takeovers leading to periods of authoritarian rule with its strutting and bemedalled presidents, sometimes, but not always, interspersed by brief intervals of impotence and anarchy miscalled democracy. Greece has been subject to domination by cliques of colonels and transient dictators. The Prussian kingdom and Bismarck's empire were bolstered by the General Staff, and even Hitler had to make his terms with the army and air force before perfecting his plans for universal

dominion. The Communist-dominated states of Eastern
Europe and their imitators in the Third World have been
ruled by colonels and field marshals and even petits caporals
modelled on Bonaparte. Indeed, remembering the Russian
Revolution when Kerensky came to power in 1917 amid
universal acclamation when I was a little boy of ten, I recall
my prescient American mother saying rather grimly in the
face of popular enthusiasm: 'Now wait for Napoleon.' And
a worse than Napoleon duly came, following the wedding
of the Communist party to the military dictatorship which
was and is the method by which authoritarian rulers maintain their dominion. Since the advent of the Napoleons of
the Soviet there has sprung up a whole brood of Gaddafis,
Saddams, Castros, Amins and whoever, each relying on an
unholy alliance between a single party, a military caste and
a secret police infiltrating the other two. Rightly, we pro-
claim the necessity of an independent judiciary as an essential condition of freedom under the rule of law. But we are
apt to forget the equal importance of armed forces equally
distanced from politics and political parties, and owing their
separate allegiance to our equally non-political and hereditary head of state. The old division of the separation of
powers into executive, judiciary and legislature is incom-
plete without this refinement. For that we owe an imperish-
able debt of gratitude to William III who established the
supremacy of parliament over the armed forces and the
judiciary, and the Hanoverian succession which, after a long
interval, gave us a non-political head of state, and a judiciary
and armed forces both of whom, despite their accountability
to parliament, owe direct allegiance not to the government
of the day but to the Sovereign. There remains one more
thing to be said, and that is to deplore the insufficient pres-
tige which attaches to the profession of arms in democratic
Britain in time of peace. Winston Churchill was never tired

of repeating the old tag which, in one form or another, goes back a long way in history:

> In the hour of danger, not before,
> God and the soldier we alike adore.
> The danger past, both are alike requited.
> God is forgotten, and the soldier slighted.

Rudyard Kipling, much derided, and sometimes not unjustly, made the same point rather less succinctly in a poem the last stanza of which runs:

> Then it's Tommy this an' Tommy that, an' 'Tommy,
> ow's yer soul?'
> But it's 'Thin red line of 'eroes' when the drums begin
> to roll.

It is a fallacy deriving, I believe, from the revulsion of feeling which followed the First World War, to suppose that the possession of strong and up-to-date armed forces in the hands of a peace-loving power is a cause of international tension and war. International tension results from international suspicion, sometimes well founded, as we know to our cost. Wars are caused by a perceived imbalance of forces in favour of a potential aggressor, as was shown by Saddam Hussein's invasion of Kuwait in 1990. The two horrible world wars in my lifetime could, I believe, have been prevented had we re-armed sufficiently and in time, if need be unilaterally. The responsibility for our failure to do so lies firmly in the deep-rooted moral irresponsibility of the intellectual establishment.

The danger has not passed. As I write I can confidently say that no one could possibly have foreseen any of the salient events of the past ten years. We have engaged in two international conflicts, the first alone and at the other end of the world, in the Falkland Islands, the second as part of an international coalition in the Gulf under the authority of the United Nations Organisation. The Soviet empire appears to have crumbled in the course of seven days. It is the unexpected that always happens. No doubt the need for fifty-five thousand troops permanently stationed in Germany as part of a NATO force has been reduced or permanently disappeared. There is currently talk of a European Community force and a Community foreign policy. What is absolutely certain is that we shall have permanent need for a flexible and well-equipped defence force with adequate reserves to protect the values in which we believe against the unexpected and undesired crises which will certainly occur from time to time. It is true, too, that we have discovered an unsurpassed and possibly unequalled formula to ensure that these forces, though accountable to parliament, shall nonetheless be independent of political pressures and patronage. We sometimes speak of the dangers of a police state. We should thank our stars that three hundred years of immunity have led us to forget the far worse dangers of a defence force tempted to interfere in policy and government.

XIII

The Police Forces and Security

THIS IS NOT a treatise on criminal law. But it would be wrong not to include a discussion of our non-political police in their role as part of our constitutional structure. Sir Robert Peel is credited, justly, with being the originator of our current system when he founded the Metropolitan Force. This he did by combining two ideas, both of which require individual scrutiny. The first was that the Metropolitan Force should combine civilian status with internal discipline. This he achieved by adapting the ancient office of constable, which possessed and still possesses certain rights over and above those of the ordinary citizen, and superimposing a hierarchical system of rank and discipline on the forces so contrived. The second was that though, uniquely because of the status of London as the capital and the location of government, the head of state and parliament, the Metropolitan Force came directly within the responsibility of government, it was never designed, nor desired, that the police forces of this country should be amalgamated into a single national body. Although from time to time forces have been rationalised by amalgamation, and the powers of constables, senior officers and bodies dealing with complaints and discipline have been reformulated by legislation, these two underlying conceptions have

66

never been altered. We cannot become a police state because we have no national police force. It cannot be pretended that this policy has never been questioned. The fact remains that it has not been disturbed.

It would be wrong, however, to claim that the system of criminal justice as enforced through the courts, invigilated by the police and underpinned by our system of prisons and other closed institutions does not constantly give rise to argument. Recently this argument has become more acute, though not necessarily better informed, because, as already mentioned, in a whole series of cases, often more than ten years after the original convictions and the dismissal of the original appeals, the Court of Appeal Criminal Division has pronounced convictions for murder and other serious offences unsafe or unsatisfactory or both after the convicted persons had spent many years in prison. The scandal is compounded by the reflection that, had the death penalty still been in place at the time of the original convictions and appeals, those convicted of murder would almost certainly not have spent the intervening years in gaol, but all or most of them would have been in their graves.

We had always prided ourselves on the reflection that our system of justice was so heavily weighted in favour of the defence that, although numerous cases might occur in which the guilty, even perversely, might be acquitted, the conviction of the innocent was, humanly speaking, an impossibility. This was, of course, not true. There was the notorious case of Adolf Beck who, in my youth, was convicted and sentenced to prison not once but on three separate occasions, on evidence which might have convinced an archangel, of some particularly mean frauds when as a matter of fact they were ultimately proved to have been committed by quite a different person. There was the less shocking, but not less disturbing, case of Oscar Slater, convicted by a

Scottish jury by a majority of eight to seven. More recently, and in England, there was the case of Doherty (another example of mistaken identity and proven innocence) and other cases of alleged false confessions or fabricated evidence which again resulted in a Home Secretary's reference, overturning a conviction otherwise than on a straightforward appeal. People ought to realise that no system of justice is infallible. But what is particularly disturbing about the more recent cases is that, whatever the outcome (some of the matters are still under investigation) some of the allegations made on the successful references rested on assertions that something had taken place which ought not to take place under any system however allegedly foolproof, namely that evidence led by the Crown on behalf of the prosecution was allegedly fabricated by those whose duty it was to bring only the guilty to the bar of justice, or that misguided scientists led expert evidence allegedly produced by some fallacious methodology. It is impossible to exaggerate the seriousness of the savage blow which this series of cases has dealt to public confidence. Much of this is misplaced and is directed either to the persons or functions of the judiciary who presided over the original trials or were parties to the dismissal of the original appeals. No system of justice is proof against fabricated or even unreliable evidence, and the jurisdiction of the Court of Appeal in criminal cases is not a rehearing of the original cause. A presiding judge on a trial on indictment is not an inquisitor but a kind of referee in the accusatorial process who is there to guide and assist juries on the intricacies of the law applicable and take them through the sometimes complicated facts and the often irrelevant or fallacious arguments of counsel. There are quite responsible and distinguished critics who would favour a move to the inquisitorial procedure almost universal on the continent, and often much misrepresented here.

This is rather like telling the Football Association and the Football League to start next season by learning the rules of American football and playing their matches by those rules. It is reassuring to know that the government has referred all this to the wisdom of a Royal Commission. But I rather wonder whether I shall live long enough to see the outcome.

I wish, therefore, to pursue a different line of reflection, based not on the undoubted scandal of unsafe or unsatisfactory convictions (or acquittals), but on more general considerations not immediately relevant to these. In passing, I pause for a moment to reflect that under the French system (not untypical of the inquisitorial procedures of the European continent) ninety-five per cent of contested trials for offences which would be tried here in the Crown Courts, result in convictions. The comparable figure in the Crown Court, varying in different parts of the country, and after the shock to public confidence caused by recent events, is nearer forty per cent. It is also worth reflecting, in view of constant and justified complaints of delays here, that the inquisitorial procedures take about three times as long to reach a final conclusion. These, however, are matters which will be considered by the Royal Commission.

What is important from the point of view of what I am now considering is that in the main the rules of procedure and evidence have not developed in step with the needs of the administration of justice or the organisation of the police.

As we all know from the stories about Sherlock Holmes, the Metropolitan Police with the stock figure of Inspector Lestrade had already been long established by the time that the tenants of the Baker Street residence had come into occupation, and survive almost intact to this day.

The rules of criminal evidence were largely developed

before the advent of Sir Robert Peel and his institution of the Metropolitan Police. It was not until 1898, by which time the Baker Street house was already occupied by its famous residents, that an accused person was even permitted to give evidence on his own behalf and be cross-examined on it. The rules of hearsay and the right of silence (labelled by Jeremy Bentham as 'the thieves' Charter') were developed in an age peopled by private prosecutors and Dogberry. It was not until 1907 that there was any general right of appeal from a verdict of conviction, and the present jurisdiction of the Court of Appeal dates only from 1968. It was not until 1989 that the Law Commission published a general report on the general principles which should govern Criminal Law and, though they accompanied their report with a Draft Bill, the coelacanths in the Home Office have done, so far as I know, absolutely nothing about it. The Police and Criminal Evidence Act of 1984 was another ad hoc measure. What is clear is that the whole system of substantive law, evidence and procedure, and the organisation of the police is a jungle of rigid and artificial rules, wrongly defined boundaries of ministerial responsibility, insufficiently coherent definitions of principle feeding a disgracefully overcrowded and consequently inhumane system of penal treatment, well intentioned but, as it stands, inadequate to contain the rising tide of crime. Here is a real field of reform requiring the services of a new Sir Robert Peel. If occasionally a misguided and frustrated police have been tempted to cut corners in a wholly indefensible manner, what has happened is in part a symptom of a far more general malady than is commonly supposed.

XIV

The Fourth Estate

IN VICTORIAN TIMES the Press was frequently referred to as the Fourth Estate, the other three being, of course, Queen, Lords and Commons. Those were the days of Tom Tower and his Thunderer, fulminating like cloud-gathering Zeus from his eyrie on the heights of Mount Olympus. Today the Fourth Estate, infinitely more influential, infinitely more pervasive, and, as I see it, considerably lower in standards, must include not only the Thunderer and the other various heavies, but the tabloids, the radio and, above all, the television. It would be idle to deny their immense power. They enter into every field of life. They tell us what to eat and drink, and what we should put on by way of raiment. They spare no one, from Royalty down. They intrude into private life. They claim to be experts on sexual and all other morality. They are accountable to almost no one, apart from a number of toothless tigers. They are bitterly resentful of criticism. Occasionally libel juries award disproportionately high damages, no doubt to express their gut reactions at the behaviour of defendants, usually the media. But, in the end, the media seem to do more or less as they please, since the remedy, censorship or regulation, is rightly viewed as a restriction on free speech. At least they remain highly competitive with one another, owned by different proprietors, appealing to different audiences, operating different vehicles of expression. That they perform indispensable functions in a parliamentary democracy is undeniable. How well, and how responsibly they perform these functions, is open to debate. Free speech is a jewel. The less political or judicial authority has to do with their performance, on the whole the better. The history of interference, by pressure groups, by religious bodies, or by parliament, is not encouraging. The fatwa, uttered by either an Attorney General or an Ayatollah, only, at least in most cases, popularises the product.

The only sanction which applies to them relatively effectively is the weight of the general law. To this, with the rest of the population, the media are equally subject. But the extent to which even this is successful as a deterrent is open to debate. I have already mentioned the laws of libel. But in my professional career I have only seldom advised resort to these or resorted to them personally. The cost, the anxiety, the delay can hardly be exaggerated. There is also the danger that the pursuit of such rights may only exaggerate the evil which it is desired to restrain. The malevolent and ridiculous fatwa pronounced by a murderous and fanatical regime against the unfortunate Salman Rushdie, and supported here by a few religious fanatics, may have made the victim's life insecure, and even unbearable, but it certainly turned his virtually unreadable book into a best-seller and, reputedly, the author himself into a millionaire. The government's attempt, far more justifiable, to restrain the publication in breach of confidence of *Spycatcher*, was hardly more successful. Many law reformers advocate a new tort action for breach of some new right to privacy. In certain countries such a right exists and is protected by law. But the success of such attempted protection is open to doubt. What is not open to doubt is that it is complicated and quite difficult to administer. The law relating to blasphemy is not an unmixed success, and the law of obscenity, though probably necessary in the light of deteriorating standards of decency at the bottom of the scale is always in danger of becoming or at least appearing absurd. The protection of ethnic and religious minorities from slander and abuse is obviously morally justifiable, but except in obvious and extreme cases is neither effective nor particularly successful in preventing discrimination. My own view of the future is somewhat bleak. I do not quite understand why the reading, listening and viewing public, who are undoubtedly shocked and disapproving, do not themselves enforce the moral standards they uphold by ceasing to patronise the publishers of offensive matter. Nor do I understand why the media themselves seem unable to impose an independent form of discipline from within. If they do not, it is quite possible that new attempts may be made to restrain them.

It is not a pretty picture. But I do not pretend to have a remedy which is not worse than the disease. The BBC, the IBA, and the Advertising Standards Authority mitigate but do not suppress the growing evil. Perhaps bad taste is the price we pay for freedom. If so, it may be worth paying. But it is, by any standards, a price which is disagreeably high.

XV

---◆◆◆---

Sovereignty: The International Dimension and The United Nations Organisation

No examination of our Constitution can avoid some discussion of the international dimensions of sovereignty, brought sharply into focus in the European aspect by the arguments of Margaret Thatcher and, in relation to international law, generally by the Gulf 'War'. It is worth while placing the discussion firmly into historical perspective.

Before 1914, the whole world was split up into a congeries of independent sovereign states, each in international law separate entities or 'legal persons'. Some possessed appendages in the form of colonies, protectorates or empires. It had been so from time immemorial, though actual powers of government had gradually drifted away from the conception of sovereign princes and emperors ruling by some fiction of divine right in favour of constitutional sovereignties acknowledging some form of internal rule of law and operating under some form of internal constitutional dispensation. Between these 'legal persons' there was an international customary 'law' of peace and an international customary 'law' of war including a customary 'law' concerning neutrality and neutrals. In some fields, these customary

laws were bolstered or supplemented by international conventions or treaties. Since much nonsense about the subject
was spoken and written, especially by ecclesiastics, during
the Gulf 'War', it is worth while reminding ourselves what
led such respected figures as St Augustine of Hippo and
St Thomas Aquinas to attempt to formulate moral rules and
criteria for sovereign princes about the criteria for 'a just
war' to restrain the irresponsible exercise of the sovereignty
of these international 'persons'. But these were moral rules
and not either in theory or practice rules of law in any
intelligible sense of the word. Indeed, it was his recognition
of this state of affairs which led my father from time to time
to claim that in the sense of a set of rules enforceable
through a structure of courts and the application of physical
sanctions there was no such thing in any real sense as international law at all, and that what passed as such was merely
a series of assertions, sometimes contradictory of one
another, by the writers of textbooks. It is true of course
that, at least since the end of the Napoleonic wars, perhaps
even since the days of Henry of Navarre, the European
world has been uneasily aware that something more effective than theological treatises was required. In fact none of
these dreams was ever realised in practice. It was the sheer
horror of the Great War of 1914–18 that changed the
scene. By 1919 it was generally realised that modern war
had become such a terrible thing that some code of conduct
capable of enforcement and regulating resort to arms by
any nation state was really essential to the continuance of
civilised life and that, for this purpose, some international
structure or institution was necessary. Such a code was
attempted and such an institution founded by the League
of Nations Covenant. As we all learned to our cost, the
attempt failed. This was partly because membership of the
new institution was never universal and in particular did not

include the United States of America, nor until 1934, by which time Germany had left, the Soviet Union. More importantly, the mechanism for enforcement proved inadequate. To prevent aggression by one state against another reliance was placed on economic sanctions rather than directly on joint military force, and these sanctions did nothing to restrain Italian aggression against Abyssinia. By that time Hitler was on the loose. It took another World War in its extent even more widespread and, in its incidents, more terrible even than that of 1914, to bring the United Nations Organisation into being. This at last explicitly accepted the need, at least in the final resort, for collective military action to restrain and prevent the use of aggression in breach of the universal code of conduct expressed in the Charter. The attempt has neither proved an unequivocal success nor a total failure. This is what gave the Gulf 'War' (the word 'war' is not strictly appropriate) its crucial significance. The occasion was the total obliteration of one member of the organisation by another without any justification whatsoever and in open defiance of the Charter. If this had been allowed to succeed without effective military action, the United Nations Organisation would have followed the League of Nations into the dustbin of history. Whatever else was achieved by the Coalition, the Security Council resolutions and the resulting military action at least prevented that. In this context, the complete irrelevance of the revered writings of St Augustine of Hippo and the Angelic Doctor about 'just wars' was obvious to all but a distinguished, learned, but singularly obtuse, minority of churchmen. Less obtuse, but equally fatuous, was the well-meant attempt to achieve the desired result by applying to the aggressive dictator nothing more effective than economic sanctions. Nevertheless, since 1945, we have left the world of independent princes restrained in their resort to force only by treaty or morality. We have undertaken to enter a new world where belligerence between sovereigns except in self-defence, or to assist the self-defence of others, is illegal in the sense that it offends a written code theoretically enforceable and applicable universally and not only to signatories to the Charter or members of the organisation. Since 1945 we have entered upon a new world order based theoretically on the rule of law policed by an institution. There are other international organisations of a character more limited, like the Helsinki Accord or the European Convention on Human Rights which prescribe limits to the treatment by signatories even of their own subjects. But, judicially speaking, 1945 was a watershed, to the consequences of which we have not yet fully accustomed ourselves. This is a fundamental change, and I therefore mention it at the outset. But it is now time to consider other international developments, intended if not expressly stated, to be permanent which are germane to our constitutional arrangements in their detailed application, and may be more far-reaching in their ultimate effect.

XVI

━━━━◆ ◆ ◆━━━━

Sovereignty:
The European
Dimension

OF ALL the numerous treaties, conventions and engagements entered into since 1945 by the United Kingdom,
the United Nations Organisation, by reason of its explicit
obligation even on non-members to observe its code of
behaviour limiting the use of force, is the most overtly
restrictive of independent national sovereignty. It is for this
precise reason that it is the sheet anchor of the new world
order into which we entered in 1945. It was his failure to
understand this which led to the humiliation of Saddam
Hussein in 1991. However ineffective the United Nations
may seem from time to time, and however nonsensical many
of its discussions, we should never allow ourselves to forget
this.

But, in day-to-day political discussion, if we partially
except the NATO alliance and the General Agreement on
Tariffs and Trade, two European organisations probably
attract more public attention. These are the European
Community and the European Convention on Human
Rights. We adhere to both. Both are intended to be indefinite in duration. Each limits the freedom of action of its
members. Technically each rates only as a treaty obligation.

In strict legal theory, I suppose that we could withdraw from either if parliament repealed any underlying statutory basis. As a matter of political reality, both are likely to continue in some form in the foreseeable future. Each raises important, and different, constitutional issues.

The first of the two to come into being was the European Convention on Human Rights. This was modelled on the Universal Declaration of Human Rights of 1948, a document of good intent, but without even the legal status of a treaty with binding effect on its adherents. This came into being as a sort of political manifesto following Hitler's atrocities before and during the Second World War. It was not designed as a legal document but as a sort of highway code signifying general guidelines which civilised societies were expected to articulate into specific laws in their domestic legislation. Unlike the Universal Declaration on which it was modelled, the European Convention has the status of a treaty binding in International Law. It is underpinned by a court supported by a commission which scrutinises and filters complaints before submission to the court, and an assembly which holds meetings for discussion but with no legislative powers. It has a wider membership than the Community and all its institutions are centralised in Strasbourg. There is no machinery for enforcement of its judgements, but members are expected to take the necessary action under their domestic law to give them effect. There is a provision under which individual litigants cannot have their complaints submitted to the court until they have exhausted their domestic remedies. Since the United Kingdom, unlike some other members, has not embodied the code in our domestic law, and so has not given British judges the right to give effect to its provisions in priority to our own laws, this has led to a disproportionately high number of complaints against the United Kingdom being admitted to the court, and, since the judges in the court are unfamiliar with British conditions, a fairly significant number of these complaints, in my own estimation some of them mistakenly, have been upheld. So far, no British government of either political persuasion has taken what I would regard as the obvious course of passing legislation providing that, in the absence of any express provision to the contrary, the law of the United Kingdom in its several parts must be read in individual cases to whatever defined extent as subject to the code. This has been due to the usual, and to my mind rather academic, discussion about sovereignty, which, in my judgement, would not, even theoretically, be infringed by a provision in this form, and would drive would-be litigants into the British courts, with British judges more familiar with British conditions, as a sort of court of first instance. Apart from the fact that, so far as I am aware, no responsible body of opinion here wishes to denounce the convention, one incidental advantage of our continued adherence is that, so long as we are members, there is an overwhelming argument against anyone concocting a new and home-brewed 'Bill of Rights' on the American model to be inserted in our domestic law. There are arguments for and against such a 'Bill of Rights'. There can be no argument in favour of having two such Bills of Rights with overlapping but differently defined 'rights' capable of conflicting with one another and giving contradictory results in individual cases. Since in practice British governments conform to the judgements of the Strasbourg court, it seems to me that there is no valid argument against the limited application I have outlined above, except, of course, that it might generate a new, and monstrous, increase in the already excessive volume of domestic litigation.

Though clearly the machinery of the European Convention to some extent foreshadowed that of the European

Community, juristically speaking our adherence to the European Community was a more revolutionary change since, so long as we remain members, the rule of the direct application in our domestic law does involve a practical limitation on the sovereign powers of parliament. For a long time our membership was held up, at first owing to internal divisions within the two main parties, but later owing to reservations, particularly by France, about our admission to membership. In the end these difficulties were overcome. Our membership was agreed and enacted in our domestic law, at first by the Act of 1972 and, later, by the Single European Act which all existing members duly ratified.

The Community developed into a single organisation out of three separate but closely allied bodies, devoted in each case to particular topics, the first Iron and Steel, the second the Atomic Energy and the third, the Economic Community.

Everything that can be said about the European Community has always been highly contentious and has remained so, ever since the subject first arose. It has already formed the subject of two fat volumes, each larger than normal, in Halsbury's *Laws of England*. The political discussion is even more voluminous and continues like a river in spate. It has already led, at least indirectly, to the precipitate loss of office of one British Prime Minister, and its ultimate effect on parliamentary, political, economic, and even constitutional life remains uncertain. One may, however, with some degree of confidence, advance certain general propositions.

In the first place, although the principal activities of the Community have, from the first, been economic, its real, but unspoken, dynamic has been political. It was born, and has thriven, on the determination of the Western European peoples after the two murderous fratricidal wars of our life-time, never to go to war again. That is what explains the almost fanatical determination of the Euro-enthusiasts not to be content with a purely economic association. If the aim had been purely economic, an association on the lines of the European Free Trade Association, now practically con-fined to former neutrals, would almost certainly have suf-ficed. If the intention had been to resist external aggression, either the almost dormant European Defence Union or NATO would have been preferable. As it is, there is a con-stant drive to economic union which continues to advance, and, in its advance, continues controversial.

So long as we remain members, as we intend indefinitely to do, our membership places limitations on our sover-eignty, and that partly but not only by the direct application to Community Law in our courts. Directives and other instruments of policy, once entered into, are meant to be obeyed by governments if by different mechanisms, and arrangements exist for enforcement by Community insti-tutions by means of legal sanctions enforceable against governments.

I do not myself see any credible British government reversing its deliberately arrived at decision to play a full part in the Community. The areas of controversy revolve around the extent to which British governments will accel-erate, or join with those anxious to restrain, the advance towards economic and political integration and the extent to which we should try to persuade the more starry-eyed of the integrationists to become outwardly rather than in-wardly looking towards the rest of the free world. To my mind at least, the original gibe of 'insularity' once levelled at the United Kingdom ('Fog in the Channel, Continent isolated') is the very reverse of the truth. The only direction in which an island people can look is outwards. It is the continentals who are inward-looking. The character of our future input into Euro-thought is more and more likely to consist in reminding the more inward-looking of our partners that there are pockets of European civilisation and culture outside Europe. 'Look,' we shall be saying, 'there is such a place as New Zealand. There is Australia. There are Canada and the United States of America. There are also vast areas of Asia and Africa which formerly were part of the British Empire and have largely adopted British institutions and often use English between indigenous but mutually unintelligible languages as their preferred lingua franca. These cannot wisely be abandoned or disregarded in framing European policy. They remain part of our heritage. We owe them friendship and, often, loyalty. Our culture, based on Christianity, is inherently outward-looking. In framing a common foreign or defence policy, these bonds cannot be disregarded, either in the interests of the members of the Community themselves or within the bounds of practical possibility, even after the demise of the Warsaw Pact and even without considering the possible consequences of the demise of the Soviet Empire.'

Another aspect of the Community to which Euro-enthusiasts will have to turn their attention is the somewhat eccentric character of the Community's structure. The European Court of Justice is in Luxembourg. The so-called parliament is hundreds of miles away in Strasbourg (the seat also of the Council of Europe). The Commission, which (despite some words to the contrary) lacks full accountability to the parliament or to anyone else but operates as a semi-independent Eurocracy, is back again, but in Brussels. The Council of Ministers, which is, I suppose, the nearest thing to an executive that the Community owns, is not responsible to the European parliament, but to the individual governments and national legislatures. Not unnaturally, the parliament itself, though directly elected, has not so far attracted the full allegiance of the several electorates, or even their real interest in its proceedings. A cynic might argue that we should not make much of our own Constitution if our courts all sat in the Strand, our parliament in Aberdeen, while the cabinet sat in Birmingham or Cardiff and its individual members owed responsibility to the leaders in our various local authorities. The inevitable result of such a structure is the considerably enhanced independence of the Eurocracy or Commission, which does not like being thought of as a civil service, whose lack of sensitivity and sense of proportion is apt to emerge from time to time in bizarre proposals attacking the legality of the British sausage, milk chocolate bars, prawn-flavoured potato crisps or the sale of giblets inside the carcass of a chicken. It remains to be seen whether and how far such a curiously balanced structure can be made workable, particularly if it is complemented by an independent central bank and a common currency, or in what sense the emergent Community can be described in any intelligible sense as a democracy. But unless some attempt, more or less successful, is made to achieve these ends it is unlikely to generate profound loyalties or warm enthusiasms.

In the meantime, this excursus into international affairs has not been without its purpose. Our preliminary examination of constitutional development since Dicey wrote has led to one or two preliminary conclusions. While Dicey's fundamental analysis which led him to found his great work on the two pillars of the Sovereignty of Parliament and the Rule of Law has remained in place, the whole fabric has become subject to increasing strains. These are largely due to the volume of activity and the degree of centralisation unavoidable in a modern state with a single national legislature endowed with unlimited powers. Parliament is asked to pass more laws than it is able to digest. More and more strain is placed on ministers. The constraints on government compel it to put more pressure on its party supporters in both Houses than is consistent with the strict theory of its accountability, and within government the same forces have placed more and more power in the hands of fewer and fewer ministers and less on the collective responsibility of the cabinet. The additional dimensions of our increasingly interdependent international responsibilities, and particularly of our Community membership, have tended to increase rather than diminish these pressures. Perhaps it is now time to look at various popular proposals for improvement.

XVII

---◆◆◆---

A Case for Regional Government?

GEOGRAPHICALLY, and in terms of population, the United Kingdom has always veered close to the maximum size which a unitary government could reasonably expect to administer. Nevertheless, we have always opted against any form of federation, and in favour of a unitary state, and of an omnicompetent and sovereign parliament. The third arm of government, the judiciary, has always been devolved between the parts. Though there is a single judicial system in England and Wales, the judiciaries of Scotland and Ireland (before 1921 and Northern Ireland since) were always separate from the English and from one another. Despite the sovereignty of the Union parliament, Scottish substantive law is not the same as that of England. The law applicable to Northern Ireland has also separate sources from English law although, due to Poyning's Act and other factors, it bears a strong family resemblance to English practice. For nearly fifty years after the Irish Treaty in 1922, despite the proximity of the South and communal differences between communities, Northern Ireland had a separate, and devolved, legislature at Stormont which did not, however, challenge the sovereignty of Westminster. When plans were being made in preparation for the last war on the assumption, which proved false, that massive aerial bombing might render government from the centre impracticable, there were contingency plans for the devolution of powers of government to regions. Shadow Commissioners were picked out and, I believe, the geographical boundaries provisionally delineated. Several Commissions or enquiries into the reform of local government since the war have looked into the possibility of the devolution of central government into regions with separate assemblies in Wales and Scotland.

It is, therefore, idle to pretend that, given my analysis that government in Westminster and Whitehall has become over-centralised, devolution of some of its powers to local assemblies in Scotland, Wales, Northern Ireland, and regions of England is either a technical impossibility or a manifest constitutional error, assuming, of course, that the underlying unity of the United Kingdom were not undermined. One Labour government after the war actually proposed devolution for Scotland and Wales, and arranged preliminary plebiscites, though in the event, both were unsuccessful, the Scottish proposal failing to achieve the necessary qualifying majority, and the Welsh not receiving a majority at all. It is idle, therefore, to pretend either that a proposal for devolution is out of the question or that, at least in some quarters, it would be devoid of a certain amount of popular support. My own party has, at least at present, turned down flatly any such schemes, primarily on the ground that it would 'put yet another tier of government on our backs', but also, I think on the ground that there is little visible support for such a suggestion in any regions of England. But the other main parties, Labour and Liberal, continue to show interest, and it must therefore be conceded that the subject is worthy of discussion.

I doubt myself whether the argument that regional government would 'put yet another tier of government on

our backs' is wholly sound. It may be granted that, in so far
as it gave regions some supervisory powers over districts,
boroughs, and countries, there is something in the objection. But, in so far as regional government might transfer
some existing central government responsibilities from
Whitehall to regional assemblies, the objection might well
be wholly misleading. On the contrary, decentralisation
from Whitehall to regional assemblies might do something
to counter the top-heaviness and over-centralisation which
has under-lain much of my argument to date. When I was
doing the work confided in me by Harold Macmillan in
1963 in the North East of England to improve employment
and economic conditions there, I had to deal with the area
comprising only the three counties of what was then the
North Riding of Yorkshire, Durham and Northumberland
with the addition of Berwick upon Tweed. I had to concern
myself with this area as a whole. I had to consider industry,
existing or to be introduced, with education, air, road, rail
and sea transport, housing, sewage disposal, ports, and
rivers. But for this I had to work in the areas of, I believe,
146 local authorities of one sort and another. Each activity
in which local authorities were interested was connected by
a separate umbilical cord to one of a whole range of minis-
tries in Whitehall, and sometimes with different officials in
the same department. I was marvellously served by a little
group of talented and carefully selected civil servants. But
the work had to continue after we had returned to London,
and, to ensure that it did, I brought into being a single
office in Newcastle where liaison could take place across the
corridors of a single building. I had in mind the precedent of
St Andrew's House in Edinburgh. But I never concealed
from myself or anyone else that my private ambition was a
regionally elected authority in Newcastle or elsewhere in
the region directly accountable to the popular electorate in

the whole area. This of course was before the Welsh and Scottish proposals of the later Labour government had been mooted, and years before our entry into the European Community added a fresh international dimension to central government activities. But, from the first, I accepted that my aim would be unachievable without similar regional local authorities, located in Scotland and Wales (Stormont, of course, then still existed in Northern Ireland), in the North West of England, the Midlands (probably centred on Birmingham), the South East (probably including Greater London), and the West Country. I was therefore disappointed when Stormont foundered, and neither the Welsh nor the Scottish proposals bore fruit.

Much has happened since 1963. There have been numerous reorganisations of local and subordinate government. None has succeeded. Stormont is in a state of cataleptic trance, with Northern Ireland governed like a Persian satrapy. The Welsh and Scottish proposals were stillborn, as, I believe, will all other proposals for Wales and Scotland unless accompanied by parallel reorganisation in the regions of England, without which the so-called West Lothian question (the ability of Scottish members to vote on English issues) will be unanswerable. The Inner London Education Authority has sunk without trace, and the Greater London Council exists only as a transient and embarrassed phantom in the form of the Transitional Authority, and with it the other semi-regional city bodies in the provinces. The Poll Tax has arrived, only to disappear like the Boojum, and has given rise to a Council Tax, to be imposed in seven, or perhaps eight or nine, layers. Various proposals have been put forward for a local income tax, obviously a non-starter with local authorities as small as Lambeth and its neighbour Wandsworth. The present proposals for a local government re-organisation seem to be based on existing councils, county, borough, or district, or a combination of two or more of them. It remains to be seen whether they will fare better than the others.

Can it be that we have failed to identify the underlying problems?

To begin with, I name but three, local government taxation, quangos (at present virtually unaccountable) and tertiary education (another problem I sought in 1963 to examine, and with some success, on a regional basis).

It is clear that a local income tax is a non-starter because of the nature of our existing local government boundaries and authorities, but it would surely be perfectly simple to assess it on a regional basis as a separate and additional imposition on present income tax returns. The quango (in my book 'quasi autonomous national governmental organisation'), unaccountable in any democratic sense, can be seen to be mainly regional in its operation. Quangos include health authorities, river and drainage undertakings, many nationalised undertakings, and many other activities which transcend local authority boundaries but have no democratic body which can monitor their activities. Welsh and Scottish nationalist leanings could be catered for, provided that separatist national pressure groups did not sabotage the idea. Tertiary education, whether at the higher or fuller levels, could fit quite conveniently into a regional pattern, provided academic independence could be assured and free trade in students guaranteed. Within the new regional structures there would be no need to adopt a ministerial system of responsibility. The committee system with some form of proportional voting and proportionate representation of the parties would suffice. The Monarchy and parliamentary sovereignty could be maintained, and no West Lothian question need arise. Though I myself would oppose any attempt to interfere with the existing House of Lords, a regionally elected second chamber in place of that House and based on the separate regions might prove the least objectionable of the various proposals for a new second chamber, although, even so, it would have to be subject ultimately to the superiority of the Commons.

All that I am saying at this stage is that regional government without diminishing parliamentary sovereignty is amongst our constitutional options, and that the case for it has perhaps not been adequately presented. It is the greatest of pities that its feasibility shows every sign of being controversial between the parties, and that my own party has come out so strongly against it.

XVIII

———— ◆◆ ————

Devolution by Function?

IN THE LAST CHAPTER I discussed the question whether the over-centralised and top-heavy nature of our present constitutional arrangements could be improved, without weakening the essential features of our traditional Constitution, by the geographical devolution of some functions of central government to regional assemblies, and decided that, for various reasons, there was a case for consideration.

But devolution need not be purely geographical. Hitherto, the arguments for or against 'privatisation' or 'contracting out' have been largely economic, based on efficiency and cheapness of operation, and the advantages or otherwise of introducing the factors of competition and a free market economy. But may there not also be a political argument based on the desirability of a reduction of the burden at the centre of things, and a reduction in the size of operational units? When the Attlee government decided to legislate to carry out the implications of the Beveridge Report after its landslide victory of 1945, they first had to dismantle a far more decentralised edifice in order to create the present structure of social services and health provision. This edifice of social provision had grown up largely higgledy piggledy, and was defective in coverage and uneven in standards of quality. The success of centralised government in time of war, and the manifest need for universalising provision in coverage and standards made it natural to centralise responsibility and destroy arrangements such as the panel system of the general practitioner service, hospital organisation, 'workman's compensation', and health provision via the 'Approved Societies'. The advantage, a universal service, free at the point of delivery, was apparent for all to see. The hidden disadvantages, rigidity, the total dependence on central funds, which had also to service all public demands for expenditure from defence, through law and order, to social security payments, to education, whether primary, secondary or tertiary, scientific research, housing and public construction, inland transport, and the nationalised industries, was less apparent at the time. But other nations have succeeded equally well and perhaps better with structures differing both in detail and often in principle from our own and the manifest disadvantages of total control at the centre, were less apparent at the time, have since become increasingly obvious in practice over the last fifty years of operation.

I sense that a different mood now prevails. In more fields than one, multiplicity of funding has come to be perceived as some guarantee of independence. I myself happen to live in a borough which has experimented, and not unsuccessfully, with contracting out even those services which were traditionally the exclusive province of direct labour. Various experimental schemes on a national scale are on foot in the fields of hospital management and school provision, and there are even suggestions that our disgraceful prison arrangements might be usefully complemented by privately run secure hostels. There is at least one successful privately run university independent wholly of public finance. In chapter three I pointed out the danger of hypostatising a rigid dualism between society and the individual and described the essentially complex structure of a free society with its intermediate entities, the 'small platoons' as they have been christened, each fitting into a complex mosaic structure, commanding different degrees of loyalty, and many performing valuable public and social services. Society is not a stark dichotomy. It is a complicated and intricate mosaic. To go into detail here would be to develop a degree of complication quite foreign to my present intentions. I believe, however, that in almost every social dimension there is a need for the political Leviathan to devolve its responsibilities downwards and enlist the funds, the activities, the enthusiasm, and the loyalties of the small platoons. For this purpose it need not sacrifice its ultimate sovereignty, its normative and invigilating responsibilities, its duty to prescribe standards and impose duties. It is not necessary, with Margaret Thatcher, to say society does not exist. But it is necessary to recognise that society is something infinitely more complex and sophisticated than is dreamed of in the philosophy of the ideological collectivist, whose 'Society' with a big 'S' is only another name for 'Serfdom'.

XIX

$\diamond\diamond\diamond$

The Legislative Process

QUITE RIGHTLY, 'obstruction' is a 'boo word'. Quite rightly, it has bad connotations. In some circles, beloved of trade unions, but not by me, 'go slow' is almost a 'hurrah word', almost a synonym for legitimate industrial action. The same thinking applies in parliament. Holding up legitimate government business without appearing to be guilty of obstruction is thought by most opposition parties to be a legitimate tactic designed to control or resist policies of which they disapprove. Their plight is that they are in a permanent minority. A frontal attack on government merely unites government supporters, fortified as they are by the closure, the guillotine, and other 'resources of civilisation' designed as a weapon against obstructionists when they go too far and seek to disrupt legitimate business. The motto of all oppositions must always be 'divide and rule'. Simply to oppose the government by moving motions of censure is not enough. 'Deny the government their legitimate business' has been the resort of oppositions from time immemorial, and we must never allow ourselves to forget that, within limits, it is a legitimate tool of defence against overbearing majorities. I must not forget that I have a natural bias towards strong governments, and that, like so many human beings, I am prone to give them credit for good intentions particularly when these coincide with my own preferences. But oppositions could never make their voices heard effectively if it were not within their power to put a spoke in the government wheel.

This chapter, however, must be written in a tone critical of the speed at which governmental wheels spin around. I submit that it is not tolerable that, year after year, governments of all political persuasions are passing three thousand pages or more of new primary legislation, almost without allowing for the wholly admirable Consolidation Acts, which make the law easier for the user to discover, and Statute Law Revision Acts which remove some of the obsolete lumber of old statute law. There must be a better way of legislating than that which we now adopt.

Some few years ago, I was honoured to be the guest of my opposite number in the French administration, the Garde des Sceaux or Keeper of the Seals. He was good enough to show me a 'projet de loi', a sort of draft Bill which he proposed to introduce into the French legislature. It was a proposal for what is known here as Legal Aid, and, making allowances for the wide differences between the concepts of the Common Law and the Code Napoléon, it covered much the same ground. I was staggered to notice that its length was not much more than a third of our own legislation designed to achieve the same purpose.

Not long afterwards, I was given a book by an English author, Sir William Dale, *Legislative Drafting: A New Approach* (Butterworths), which established that the same phenomenon was not just true generally of French legislators, but of nearly all continental countries. The author had chosen various subjects, one, I recollect, was family law, in which different systems were compared with our own and he established quite conclusively that our continental neighbours enacted statutes in each case between a fifth and a third as long as we had done. Given my diagnosis that our whole constitutional system is overburdened at the centre, and my experience of hours of my life wasted in waiting for divisions in interminable debates on subjects of which I knew little and was even less interested, I came to the conclusion that there is something wrong in our present system of passing legislation which comprises introduction and first reading, second reading, committee and report at which amendments (in the Lords, unlimited,) can be proposed, third reading (with, in the Lords, still further opportunities to amend), and in the end an Act five times as long as French or Swedish legislation to the same effect. I do not pretend to have a solution to the problem, but I still think that we could do better. At any rate, the questions raised cannot be wholly ignored.

My first target would be the rules of construing statute law adopted by the courts. All constitutional countries adopt the principle that, in interpreting legislation, the courts are bound to give effect to the perceived intentions of their legislatures or parliaments. But the rule of construction in the English courts has been that this intention is to be found primarily in the grammatical meaning of the words in the Act. If these are capable of only one meaning, unless the words are incomprehensible or ingenuity can discover more than one possible interpretation, the courts are bound by it, even if the result defies common sense. In recent years, the courts have shown an increasing tendency to adopt a more 'purposive' construction to Acts in order to avoid absurd results, and, for this purpose, to return to an earlier doctrine to search out what is called the 'mischief of the Act', that is, to discover its purpose and to give if they can be stretched so far, a meaning conformable to that purpose. In the main, however, precedent is too strong for the courts to go very far down the road without a deliberate alteration of the rules. This has led to great prolixity in the drafting of our statutes, aided and abetted by the late Lord Hewart's hatred of secondary legislation as expressed in his *New Despotism,* and by the passion of all oppositions and pressure groups to insert a mass of words 'on the face of the Act' to underline the obvious.

Now, it was my experience in the war in dealing with a French civil administration operating side by side with us in the Lebanon, and on reading the projet de loi on legal aid as designed by my friend the Garde des Sceaux in Paris, that the French at least adopt a very different attitude. They adopt the broad line that the general purpose of a piece of legislation should be very plainly stated at the outset, and that, subject to the control of the courts, the executive should be given a great deal more freedom than is popular here, to give effect to the purpose of the Act. The result is a great deal less verbiage in both primary and secondary drafting and, I would guess, a much firmer hold on the executive to prevent its fudging the issues to its own advantage.

In the book to which I have referred, Sir William Dale examines the legislative processes in France, West Germany and Sweden, all of which share a certain family resemblance and have the same main characteristics, which are different from ours. In none of them is there the same procedure as our own. We begin with preliminary battles between the departments for a place in the programme. We then seek ministerial approval for drafting instructions to Parliamentary Counsel, and a mention in the Queen's Speech. There follows formal introduction into parliament, then the passage through each House by the processes I have outlined, from first reading to third. Finally the finished product must be interpreted and applied by the courts following the canons of construction already described.

Sir William Dale may, of course, be wrong, but I cannot forbear to quote what he says about the final product in France (op. cit. p. 87):

> Statutory Law in France has an order, a logical develop-
> ment, a freshness, a certain elegance, missing from ours.
> There is an absence of unfamiliar language, and a purity
> of expression, and an overall quality of readability.

I cannot improve on this, and I cannot resist reflecting sadly upon his conclusion about our own standard in the finished product (ibid. p. 331):

> Features making for obscurity or length, usually both, in
> United Kingdom Acts are:
> a) long involved sentences and sections;
> b) much detail, little principle;
> c) an indirect approach to the subject matter;
> d) subtraction as in 'subject to' ... 'provided that';
> e) centrifugence (a flight from the centre) to defi-
>   nition and interpretation clauses;
> f) poor arrangement;
> g) schedules – too many and too long;
> h) cross references to other Acts – saving space, but
>   increasing vexation.
>
> In contrast, lucid and often succinct drafting is to be
> found in the countries on the European continent rep-
> resented in this study by France, Germany and Sweden.

One of the delaying features in our drafting and legislative process is the intervention of preliminary scrutinies of the draft including scrutiny by all-party parliamentary commit-tees before the Bill is submitted to parliament for en-actment.

It is now more than ten years since the publication of Sir William Dale's book and virtually nothing has been done to improve things. My own view is that the time has come, preferably by a committee of both Houses, to examine every aspect and all stages of the legislative process. The object of the exercise would be to produce better quality Bills before introduction, shorter processes of debate, and better quality and more concise laws on presentation for Royal Assent. For this purpose, the enquiry would have to cover the canons adopted by the courts for the interpretation of Statutes, a procedure producing draft Bills for scrutiny by parliament before formal introduction and finally the parliamentary procedures by which bills could be adequately discussed and amended during their passage through parliament. Our present legislative procedures I believe to be inadequate, unduly prolonged in time, restrictive of adequate debate on questions of principle as well as encouraging excessive prolixity in drafting.

XX

———◆◆◆———

Diversification

THE PROCESS of over-centralisation which I have been
trying to describe had been going on steadily, but largely
unnoticed, since the turn of the century. But the real watershed was the Labour landslide of 1945. I well remember
the euphoria which led up to this. Ever since the publication
of the Beveridge Report which more or less coincided with
the assurance of coming victory given by the twin triumphs
at Alamein and Stalingrad, a sort of starry-eyed idealism
prophesied a new world, or at least a new Britain following
the end of the war, by that time already foreseen as a cer-
tainty.

To some extent I went along with this idealism at the
time. I do not think I was entirely wrong. I have always
attributed the scale if not the fact of the Labour victory to
the largely negative response of the Conservative component of the coalition government to the Beveridge
Report when it came out. In itself the report was a fairly
modest document. It pointed firmly to the inadequacies of
the embryonic, limited and complicated social services of
the time, advocated a policy designed to reduce unemploy-
ment to ten per cent at the then current method of compu-
tation and presaged a universal system of health care to be

available free of charge at the point of delivery to take the place of the old panel system, 'Approved Societies' and variously organised hospitals. My formula at the time was 'publicly organised social services and privately owned industry'. The attitude of the Labour Party, elated, with a landslide victory in 1945, was altogether more euphoric. Wearing the uniform of my own regiment, John Freeman moved the adoption of the address at the opening of the new parliament with the phrase: 'D-Day in the battle for the New Britain'. Though there was much that was well-intentioned and genuinely idealistic in the measures of the Attlee government, the reality hardly turned out quite as people had hoped.

Attlee himself will go down in history as the Truman of British politics. Both men succeeded political giants. Each did better than anyone would have prophesied. But the Attlee government made the choice of Socialist planning at the centre. In the industrial field this took the form of a first and grandiose step towards the implementation of Clause 4 of the still unaltered Labour Constitution, that is, 'the common ownership of *all* the means of production, distribution and exchange'. The formula for achieving this was the setting up of a central quango subject to political instruction but independent at the operational level, and, as presaged in Clause 4, the promise of a new 'shopping list' every time a new Labour government was elected to office as a result of the so-called swing of the pendulum. I believe this to have been an unmitigated disaster, and a principal cause of the top-heavy government structure and over-centralisation in Whitehall from which we now suffer. In the field of Welfare, the pattern was similar in direction but less disastrous in practice. The new system for education had already been put in place by R. A. Butler during the coalition period and showed a more sensitive and diversified approach, and the disastrous era of attempted universal comprehensivisation under subsequent Labour administrations was yet to come. In health, the Beveridge Report, although not dealing with the subject specifically, had indicated quite clearly that pre-war provision of health services was neither adequate in range of treatment available, nor sufficiently universal in scope to provide adequate provision. But tastes and needs differ. When Aneurin Bevan inherited the duty of designing the Health Service, there was already in existence a network of Trade Union and insurance based 'Approved Societies' which, universalised, and still further diversified, could almost certainly have delivered a universal service, free at the point of delivery, and offering a wide range of different types of treatment and service. Other European countries have demonstrated that there are more ways than one of achieving the same end, without reducing the amount of public finance available for health care. The doctrine of the day, that 'the man in Whitehall is always right', contained an element of truth which was far short of the whole truth, and so, in place of diversification, flexibility and multiplicity of funding, with organisations accountable at regional level and the possibility of optional extras, the public was given a uniform, centralised, and sometimes inefficient system whose defects we are only now beginning to discover and from whose limitations we are only now seeking to break free. Tertiary education, prior to the Robbins report, and without adequate regional backing, was at first kept behind by the Treasury as a kind of private spending vice, separately funded and secretly indulged in. The impenetrable jungle of social security benefits is still being argued over. What emerged was not all bad and was almost certainly better than the somewhat higgledy-piggledy arrangements which had existed on an inadequate scale before the war. But the new system's philosophy was doctrinaire and

over-centralised, and its financing unimaginative and destructive of wealth.

The road forward must be to diversify and decentralise
functions. There are many ways of doing this. Diversification may take the form of geographical devolution to
regions. It may take the form of privatisation or contracting
out. Its object must always be the same, to increase flexibility and range of choice, and to reduce the reliance of the
system on a musclebound bureaucracy at the centre.

XXI

◆◆◆

Final Thoughts

THIS BOOK is founded on two premises. The first is that our traditional Constitution though essentially sound is now under strain, and that therefore reform is properly on the agenda. The second is that patent medicines do not work, and that we should therefore beware of anything which subtracts from the essential ingredients which have made our traditional Constitution among the most successful in the world. The essential ingredients are a strong executive based on an omnicompetent and elective legislature controlled by the necessity to call regular elections, by a powerful and independent opposition ready to take over, and limited more often by convention and precedent than by rules of law, and regulated more by checks and balances deriving from political constraints and necessities than by a written legal code policed by a Supreme Court. This is why, at the beginning, I called this, with a small 'c', a conservative book. It eschews written Constitutions, patent methods of voting, 'charters' or Bills of Rights. In using these terms I do not mean to condemn the fashionable habit of political parties labelling their political manifestos in particular fields as 'charters', so long as these are understood as manifestos and nothing else. I am aiming at 'Charter 88', 'Bill of Rights' (in the American sense) and the like.

I do not wish to monkey about with the Monarchy (our name for our hereditary method of identifying the legitimate head of state). I do not wish to create a rival to the House of Commons in an elective House of Lords (though the boundaries are not sacrosanct) and I do not wish to make fundamental changes in the responsibilities of our principal officers of state.

This does not mean that the agenda will not prove extensive. It is necessary to cover the whole field of policy. Objective analysis reveals that the source of constitutional malaise lies in the vastly increased activity of the modern state in almost every field of activity from legislation, international involvement, economic policy and finance right down to the minutest details of regulations and local government. The remedy may be complex. It will involve doing less where this is possible, diversifying wherever appropriate, multiplying the sources of finance, devolving, contracting out, to legislating more efficiently, and wherever possible, more concisely, restoring collegiality to the cabinet, and generally reducing the concentration on the centre. In short, we must reduce the number of areas in which individuals, the 'small platoons', and regional communities feel themselves constrained and alienated. Above all we must never lose sight of 'value judgments' in the organisation of public affairs. This applies to law, to the details of traffic regulation, to 'codes of practice', to our care for the environment. Law is only morality, honesty, decency, respect for beauty, humanity, and justice between individuals, translated into the enforceable, expressed in terms of the normative, and limited by common sense. Lose sight of these things and we are lost.